WHEN USING KITCHEN APPLIANCES PLEASE ALWAYS FOLLOW
THE MANUFACTURER'S INSTRUCTIONS

HarperCollins*Publishers*
1 London Bridge Street
London SE1 9GF

www.harpercollins.co.uk

HarperCollins*Publishers*
Macken House, 39/40 Mayor Street Upper
Dublin 1, D01 C9W8, Ireland

First published by HarperCollins*Publishers* 2023

3 5 7 9 10 8 6 4 2

A catalogue record of this book is available from the British Library

ISBN 978-0-00-856769-9

Design by Lynnette Eve at Design Jam

Photographer: Sam Folan
Food Stylist: Pippa Leon and Lauren Becker
Prop Stylist: Lauren Miller

Printed and bound by GPS

MIX
Paper from
responsible sources
FSC™ C007454

FSC
www.fsc.org

This book is produced from independently certified FSC™ paper
to ensure responsible forest management.

For more information visit: www.harpercollins.co.uk/green

Sarah Rossi

WHAT'S FOR DINNER?

Fuss-free family food in 30 minutes

HarperCollins*Publishers*

CONTENTS

INTRODUCTION

INTRODUCTION

I started writing my blog, *Taming Twins*, in 2013, with the intention of writing about life with my children, but it quickly evolved into me sharing recipes and meal ideas. It was an escape, something for me, and a way of nurturing my life-long love of food, rather than being totally consumed by being Mum.

People often ask me about my love of cooking. The truth is, I'm not sure if I do really love cooking, but I certainly love eating. All memories of important moments in my life include food: the Digestive biscuits that the kind nurse gave me after I'd just given birth; crumbs on the blue blanket as I snapped them in half and realised that life would never be the same again. Or when there's a pang of missing my father. I often think of him in the kitchen on a weekend morning, frying potatoes (skin on, smothered in salt) with a side of advice on life, and I wonder, what words of wisdom he would be serving me now? Then, there was the Béarnaise sauce that my husband so lovingly made for me on our fifth date. It was so buttery that I wiped every last bit from the bowl with a stray chip, and thought that perhaps I should, in fact, marry him at some point. Or the memory of the finely chopped Greek salad that I ate with a spoon the night that I celebrated being asked to write this book.

And so, there's always food, but sometimes life gets in the way, so I've written this book for everyone who, like me, loves to eat but can't always manage to find the energy to think about what to cook.

Sarah

HOW TO USE THIS BOOK

This book includes Meal Plans for 10 weeks. The idea is you select a daily/weekly plan to save the mental load of having to think about what to make for the week ahead. Use the shopping list for your groceries the weekend before, and you're good to go. Of course, you don't have to stick to the meal plans, and you can vary them to suit your own family's tastes.

If you're using the shopping lists dont forget to check your cupboards and fridge to see what you already have before you go shopping.

The recipes in the book are also organised in chapters, split by ingredient and meal type, so you can cook individual recipes and return to your favourites.

THE RECIPES

01

Each dinner is a complete meal and is ready in 30 minutes.

02

Every recipe has been written to cater for family friendly tastes.

03

No huge ingredient lists.

THE MEAL PLANS

01

Each week includes
6 dinners (2 per week with sides),
1 weekend breakfast
and 1 sweet treat.

02

There's a handy shopping list for each week showing you exactly what you need to buy.

03

Each week includes 1 vegetarian meal, at least 1 fish dish, a good variety of different carbs and proteins.

WHY ONLY SIX DINNERS?

In the meal plans I've included six dinners, rather than seven, a meal for every evening apart from one, just because I think we need to include a little flexibility in our lives and to make the Meal Plans perhaps more achievable for all. (Yes, you can read between the lines here – every time I've ever planned a week's worth of dinners, I've failed to cook them all, then lost my way altogether!) Let's be kind to ourselves.

A few options for dinner number seven:

★ **BAKED POTATOES**
Choose your own favourite topping. The ultimate comfort food!

★ **A MEAL FROM THE FREEZER**
– see page 12 for options.

★ **LEFTOVERS**
From the week – a single recipe or a mixture of dishes.

★ **SUNDAY ROAST**
Choose your favourite, vegetarian or not.

★ **NO-COOK NIGHT**
Cooked meat, bread and salads.

MEALS TO SUIT YOUR MOOD

Meals for when your budget is tight
– 20-minute Beef Stroganoff Pasta (*p.88*)
– Cheat's Tortilla Pizzas (*p.96*)
– Quick Tuna & Pea Patties (*p.160*)
– Sticky Turkey Tacos (*p.156*)
– Sausage & Mash with a Secret (*p.120*)

Meals for when you need comfort
– Hotpot in a Hurry (*p.124*)
– Bacon & Corn Chowder (*p.144*)
– Get Well Soon Soup (*p.52*)
– Sausage Spaghetti with Spinach (*p.90*)
– Broccoli & Bacon Bake (*p.132*)

Meals for when you can't face cooking
– Storecupboard Spaghetti (*p.72*)
– 15-minute Fish Tacos (*p.140*)
– Speedy Smash Burgers (*p.176*)
– 15-minute 'BLT' Pasta (*p.82*)
– Chicken Tikka-style Naan Burgers (*p.184*)

Meals to make double and freeze
– Chickpea Peanut Butter Curry (*p.62*)
– One-pan Lasagne (*p.80*)
– Pot Pie in a Pinch (*p.102*)
– Cauliflower Cheese Soup (*p.54*)
– Lazy Lamb Tagine (*p.116*)

Meals for when you want to impress
– One-pot Lamb Orzo (*p.84*)
– Coconut Curried Salmon (*p.100*)
– Crunchy Cutlets (*p.104*)
– Sticky Gammon Steaks (*p.126*)
– Crispy Salmon with Pineapple Salsa (*p.164*)

TIPS FOR SAVING TIME & MONEY IN THE KITCHEN

You can buy chopped fresh onions, garlic and ginger to save time, but they do go off quickly. I prefer to buy them all pre-chopped but frozen as they last so much longer.

Jars/tubes of garlic or ginger pre-prepared are a good option but may contain preservatives, so watch out for too many additives. They can also be more expensive than frozen. Alternatively, chop your own in bulk when you have some spare time and freeze.

Invest in a meat thermometer (I like the Thermopen brand). This means you can cook meat and poultry (especially useful with chicken breasts) just enough, so they are safe to eat, but not overcooked, also saving time – win win.

Buy a good-quality, large, deep frying pan (sometimes called a sauté pan) with a lid (see page 15). It has a wider surface area than a saucepan, plus a lid to keep the heat in, which equals quicker cooking times. Always use the right size pan for the quantity of food you are cooking.

£

Some frozen fruit and vegetables are cheaper to buy than fresh, and because they last longer you can reduce the risk of food waste. It's always worth checking before buying if you're budgeting. It is also worth remembering that frozen food can often be better quality than fresh as it's frozen soon after picking.

£

Cook double the recipe quantity and freeze the extra portion whenever you can – there's a list of suggested recipes to refer to (see page 12). This allows you to save energy and buy ingredients in bulk or seasonally, which is often cheaper.

£

Make a list and don't go shopping when you're hungry to avoid impulse buying. I know these are the oldest tricks in the book, but they do work.

£

Make full use of your oven each time it's used. Several of the recipes in this book are served with a side dish that can be cooked in the oven at the same time as the main. You could also use a spare shelf in the oven while it's on to throw in some potatoes to bake, then re-heat them in the microwave the next day for a quick lunch.

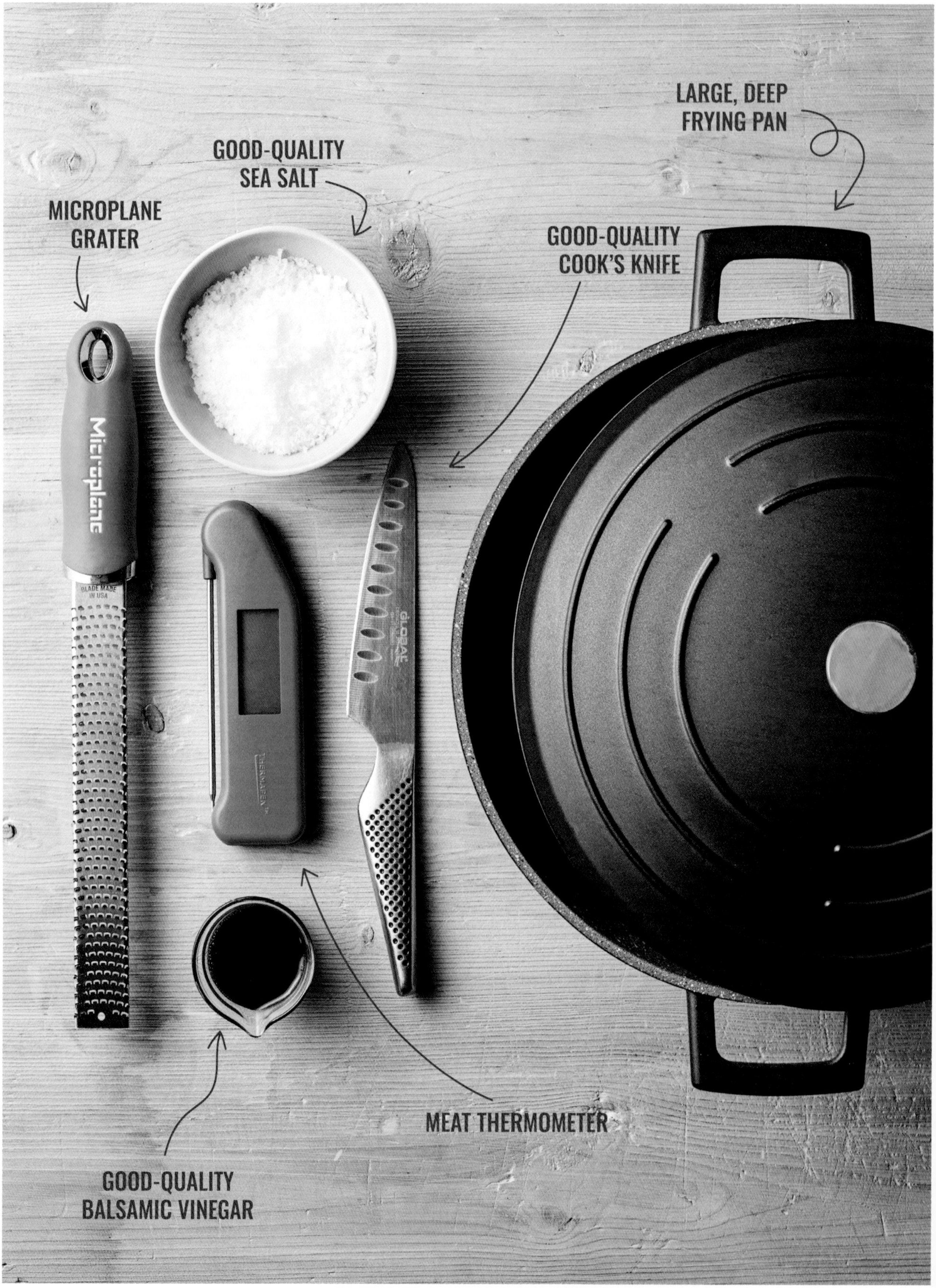

MICROPLANE
GRATER

GOOD-QUALITY
SEA SALT

LARGE, DEEP
FRYING PAN

GOOD-QUALITY
COOK'S KNIFE

MEAT THERMOMETER

GOOD-QUALITY
BALSAMIC VINEGAR

KITCHEN EQUIPMENT & INGREDIENTS WORTH SPENDING MONEY ON

- **Large, deep frying pan** (often called a sauté pan) with a lid (see page 13) – choose one that is also ovenproof and can be used under a grill. It doesn't need to be expensive but, as always, I would suggest buying the best quality you can afford so that it lasts longer.

- **Meat thermometer** – this simple utensil is the sure-fire way to know when your meat is cooked, without over- or under-cooking it. Using a meat thermometer is also incredibly helpful when you are trying to cook quickly as it removes any indecisiveness: 'Oh I'll give it another 10 minutes just in case'. I like the Thermopen brand.

- **Microplane grater** – these are very fine, very sharp graters. I avoided using lemon zest in a recipe before I owned one of these as zesting was such a faff. These are very much worth the money, and last for years. They also grate cheese (especially Parmesan) like nothing else – they use magic to make it go further than you'd think possible! They are also, handy for grating garlic and ginger, if you can't face chopping it.

- **A good-quality cook's knife** – one decent knife is, in my opinion, far more useful than a whole block of mediocre kitchen knives. I like a Global 13cm GS-51 knife, although that's not to say it's the best knife for you, but it fits well in my hand and has lasted about 15 years so far – and is still going strong. Shop to your own budget for a knife that feels weighty enough in your hand to be reliable and comfortable to last.

- **Good-quality sea salt and balsamic vinegar** – can I lump these ingredients together here? They are two foods I do think it's worth spending money on if you can. I like Maldon sea salt flakes and the Gift of Oil brand of balsamic vinegar (available via mail order). Both ingredients will improve the taste of your cooking with minimal effort.

A FEW THOUGHTS BEFORE WE GET COOKING...

A NOTE ON 'FAMILY'

I've always written about what I call 'family' food as my recipes tend to meet the needs of parents cooking for children. Too often the image of a 'family' has been portrayed in the media as a nuclear 2.4 children with 2 parents, yet I am very aware, my own life included, that this often isn't the case. So, when writing this book, I've had in mind families of all shapes and sizes.

I've had to choose a standard size for the meals, so while they all serve 4, they can easily be adapted, and leftovers can make an excellent lunch or dinner the next day, or frozen until needed. Whether you're cooking for two, four, sharing dinner with grateful housemates or are a single parent juggling cooking meals on your own, I hope this book helps YOUR own unique family unit, however that looks.

A NOTE ON THE ORIGIN OF RECIPES

Over the last year, I've been thinking a lot about how my recipes are influenced by other cultures and how I can be more respectful of this. Honestly, I don't always get this right, but I'm working on it. My first step is to educate myself about the cultures that inspire our cooking and using my platform to amplify those creators who are doing brilliant work to share their food culture with us.

I wanted to include a list of cookery books that have inspired me as I learn more about our food influences. I hope you hunt some of them out to learn more too:

- *MEZCLA, Recipes to Excite*, Ixta Belfrage *(Ebury Press).*

- *Dishoom*, Shamil Thakrar *(Bloomsbury Publishing).*

- *Fresh India: 130 Quick, Easy and Delicious Vegetarian Recipes for Every Day*, Meera Sodha *(Fig Tree).*

- *Ciudad de Mexico: Recipes and Stories from the Heart of Mexico City*, Edson Diaz Fuentes *(Hardie Grant UK).*

- *Made in Italy: Food & Stories* Giorgio Locatelli *(Fourth Estate).*

- *The Spanish Home Kitchen: Simple, Seasonal Recipes and Memories from My Home*, José Pizarro *(Hardie Grant UK).*

- *Asma's Indian Kitchen*, Asma Khan *(Pavilion).*

- *Persiana*, Sabrina Ghayour *(Mitchell Beazley).*

- *Taverna*, Georgina Hayden *(Square Peg).*

INGREDIENT NOTES & STORECUPBOARD ITEMS

Olive oil: Use basic olive oil for cooking. Don't use extra virgin as it will burn and it's also a waste of money to cook with as you won't notice the flavour.

Garlic granules: These are a dried garlic and a very useful shortcut sometimes. If you can only find garlic powder (a finer ground version) this is almost always fine to use. Don't confuse with garlic salt, which unsurprisingly, is very salty!

Eggs: Unless otherwise stated, these are medium sized.

Butter: Recipes usually state salted or unsalted. I tend to be quite forgiving about this and I wouldn't let not having the right type of butter stop me using a recipe (assuming you don't mind a savoury salt tang in baked goods). Please don't substitute with margarine of any kind though.

Onions/garlic/ginger: I often substitute these for the pre-chopped frozen versions which are very handy. Unless they are going into a salad or being eaten raw, this substitution almost always works well.

Size of vegetables: Obviously the size of vegetables can vary a lot and sometimes you'll need to use your own judgment. Unless otherwise stated recipes use a medium-sized onion of about 190g in peeled weight. If yours are small, just use more to achieve a similar weight.

Here is a list of the items you'll see regularly on the storecupboard section of the shopping lists in this book, in case you want to stock up. Don't feel you need to, but this is here if you do want to be super organised.

BASICS
- Beef stock cubes
- Chicken stock cubes
- Vegetable stock cubes
- Sea salt and black pepper
- Cornflour
- Olive oil
- Sunflower oil
- Tomato purée

DRY SPICES
- Chinese 5-spice
- Dried mixed Italian herbs
- Dried oregano*
- Dried parsley
- Dried sage
- Dried thyme
- English mustard powder

- Fennel seeds
- Garam masala
- Garlic granules*
- Ground cinnamon
- Ground coriander
- Ground cumin*
- Ground ginger
- Ground turmeric
- Paprika*
- Ras el hanout spice mix
- Smoked paprika
- Sweet smoked paprika
- Cajun seasoning*
- Cayenne pepper
- Mixed spice
- Tikka spice mix
- Curry powder*
- Onion powder

SAUCES AND JARS
- Chilli sauce
- Sweet chilli sauce
- Cider vinegar
- Soy sauce
- Dark soy sauce
- Runny honey
- American mustard
- Balsamic vinegar
- Dijon mustard
- Wholegrain mustard
- Hoisin sauce
- Mint sauce (the vinegary type, not mint jelly)
- Tomato ketchup
- Green pesto
- Oyster sauce
- Worcestershire sauce

- White wine vinegar
- Mango chutney
- Marmalade
- Jam
- Jalapeños (from a jar)

BAKING
- Golden syrup
- Baking powder
- Cocoa powder
- Vanilla extract
- Soft dark brown sugar
- Soft light brown sugar
- Caster sugar
- Icing sugar
- Plain flour
- Self-raising flour

* If you don't want to buy too many spices, start with just these.

WEEK 1: SHOPPING LIST

FRUIT & VEG

- ○ 1 onion*
- ○ ½ red onion
- ○ 6 spring onions
- ○ 11 garlic cloves*
- ○ 1kg potatoes (Maris Piper if possible)
- ○ 5 carrots
- ○ ¼ red cabbage (use the rest to make lunchtime salads)
- ○ 250g Savoy cabbage
- ○ 2 celery sticks (use the rest cut into sticks for snacks during the week)
- ○ 150g sugar snap peas
- ○ 200g long-stem broccoli
- ○ 2 red peppers
- ○ 2 courgettes
- ○ 1 avocado (for the burgers)
- ○ Tomatoes (for the burgers)
- ○ Lettuce (to go in the burgers)
- ○ 100g cherry tomatoes
- ○ 4 limes
- ○ 3 lemons
- ○ 1 apple (if you buy a pack, use the rest as snacks)

MEAT/FISH

- ○ 400g turkey steaks
- ○ 600g skinless, boneless chicken breasts
- ○ 500g lean beef mince
- ○ 500g pork mince
- ○ 90g prosciutto (about 6 thin slices)
- ○ 4 cod fillets (about 500g in total)*
- ○ 120g ham, about 8 thin slices

FRIDGE/FREEZER

- ○ 100ml whole milk
- ○ 100g unsalted butter
- ○ 100g Greek yoghurt
- ○ 150g garlic and herb cream cheese
- ○ 250g cream cheese
- ○ 200g fresh tomato salsa
- ○ 80g mature Cheddar cheese

- ○ 75g Parmesan cheese
- ○ 75g mayonnaise
- ○ 150g frozen peas

EVERYTHING ELSE

- ○ 1 x 400g tin chopped tomatoes
- ○ 1 x 325g tin sweetcorn
- ○ 1 x 400g tin black beans
- ○ 2 x 250g microwave rice pouches (or regular rice if you prefer)
- ○ 250g dried pasta
- ○ 300g fresh, ambient or frozen tortellini
- ○ 250g dried medium egg noodles
- ○ 125g rolled oats
- ○ 50g walnuts
- ○ 75g milk or plain chocolate
- ○ 4 burger buns
- ○ 9 eggs

STORECUPBOARD

- ○ Sea salt and black pepper
- ○ Sunflower oil
- ○ Olive oil
- ○ Sweet smoked paprika
- ○ Ground cumin
- ○ Dried sage
- ○ Chinese 5-spice
- ○ Paprika
- ○ Soy sauce (optional)
- ○ Wholegrain mustard
- ○ Cornflour
- ○ Runny honey
- ○ Baking powder
- ○ Ground cinnamon
- ○ Vanilla extract
- ○ Tomato purée
- ○ Hoisin sauce
- ○ Vegetable stock cubes
- ○ Pesto
- ○ Soft light brown sugar
- ○ Plain flour

Buy frozen if you prefer

MONDAY

Chunky Tortellini Soup *(p. 64)*

TUESDAY

Naked Burrito Rice *(p. 148)*

WEDNESDAY

Honey & Lime Turkey Noodle Bowl *(p. 152)*

THURSDAY

Pork & Apple Burgers *(p. 180)*
Rainbow Coleslaw *(p. 183)*

FRIDAY

Crispy Pesto Cod *(p. 154)*
Garlic & Herb Mash *(p. 158)*

SATURDAY

15-minute Paprika Chicken Pasta *(p. 92)*

WEEKEND BREAKFAST

Egg Muffin Cups *(p. 44)*

TREATS

Oatmeal Chunk Cookies *(p. 192)*

MONDAY

Four-cheese Frittata *(p. 58)*
Green Goodness Salad *(p. 57)*

TUESDAY

15-Minute 'BLT' Pasta
(p. 82)

WEDNESDAY

Build-Your-Own Burrito Bowls
(p. 142)

THURSDAY

Peanut Pork Noodles
(p. 98)

FRIDAY

One-pot Lamb Orzo
(p. 84)

SATURDAY

Quick Tuna & Pea Patties *(p. 160)*
Speedy Sweet Potato Fries
(p. 159)

WEEKEND BREAKFAST

Very Berry Baked Oats *(p. 32)*

TREATS

Cheat's Danish Pastries *(p. 196)*

WEEK 2: SHOPPING LIST

FRUIT & VEG
- 2 onions*
- 1 red onion (you can use brown onions if you prefer)
- 10 spring onions
- 1 garlic clove*
- 750g new potatoes
- 1kg sweet potatoes (about 4 medium)
- 300g cherry tomatoes
- 1 head of lettuce (I like romaine or butterhead)
- 3 green peppers
- 2 red peppers
- 1 punnet of cress
- 2 avocados
- 180g baby spinach leaves
- 150g baby sweetcorn
- 2 lemons
- 4 limes
- 260g mixed berries (blueberries and raspberries work well)*
- 200g raspberries

MEAT/FISH
- 200g smoked bacon lardons
- 500g lamb mince
- 400g boneless pork loins
- 500g skinless, boneless chicken breasts

FRIDGE/FREEZER
- 160ml milk of your choice
- 200g Greek yoghurt
- 300ml crème fraîche
- 375g ready-rolled puff pastry
- 100g soft goat's cheese
- 100g mozzarella cheese
- 100g Parmesan cheese
- 50g mature Cheddar (check the recipe notes for the cheeses, as you can use up other cheese here)
- 100g feta cheese (optional)
- 400g frozen peas
- 200g fresh tomato salsa (from the supermarket dips section)

EVERYTHING ELSE
- 2 x 145g tins tuna chunks in brine
- 1 x 325g tin sweetcorn
- 1 x 400g tin black beans
- 300g dried pasta
- 250g dried orzo
- 250g dried medium egg noodles
- 2 x 250g microwave rice pouches (or regular rice if you have time)
- 160g rolled oats
- 50g roasted peanuts
- 150g smooth peanut butter
- 25g flaked almonds
- 100g tortilla chips
- 14 eggs

STORECUPBOARD
- Sea salt and black pepper
- Sunflower oil
- Olive oil
- Runny honey
- Cider vinegar
- Wholegrain mustard
- Ground cumin
- Dried oregano
- Garlic granules
- Sweet smoked paprika
- Cajun seasoning
- Vegetable stock cubes
- Mint sauce (the vinegary type, not mint jelly)
- Soy sauce
- Tomato purée
- Baking powder
- Ground cinnamon
- Jam
- Plain flour

* Buy frozen if you prefer

WEEK 3: SHOPPING LIST

FRUIT & VEG
- ○ 2 onions*
- ○ 2 red onions
- ○ 4 garlic cloves*
- ○ 500g new potatoes
- ○ 3 celery sticks
- ○ 150g chestnut mushrooms
- ○ 1 aubergine
- ○ ½ red cabbage (use leftovers for lunchtime salads)
- ○ 180g baby spinach leaves
- ○ 2 green peppers
- ○ 4 corn on the cob
- ○ 2 large tomatoes
- ○ 1 avocado
- ○ 2 apples (use the rest of the bag for snacks)
- ○ 1 lemon
- ○ 3 limes
- ○ Fresh basil (optional)

MEAT/FISH
- ○ 400g sausages (about 6)
- ○ 4 bacon rashers
- ○ 500g lean beef mince
- ○ 225g chorizo ← *the type in a ring*
- ○ 600g skinless, boneless chicken breasts
- ○ 500g white fish fillets, without skin (you could use frozen and defrost if you prefer)
- ○ 4 pork loin fillets (about 600g in total)

FRIDGE/FREEZER
- ○ 50g butter
- ○ 4 slices of mature Cheddar cheese
- ○ 200g Parmesan cheese
- ○ 250g garlic and herb cream cheese
- ○ 200g frozen peas
- ○ 150g natural yoghurt
- ○ 75g Greek yoghurt
- ○ 70g mayonnaise

EVERYTHING ELSE
- ○ 2 x 400g tins chickpeas
- ○ 1 x 400ml tin coconut milk
- ○ 2 x 400g tin chopped tomatoes
- ○ 150g sun-dried tomatoes in oil
- ○ 1 x 397g tin condensed milk
- ○ 400g milk chocolate
- ○ 125g pretzels
- ○ 100g peanut butter
- ○ 300g arborio risotto rice
- ○ 250g dried pasta
- ○ 4 burger buns, such as brioche
- ○ 8 small tortilla wraps
- ○ 75g dried breadcrumbs *I like Panko*
- ○ 50g walnuts
- ○ 6 large eggs
- ○ 300g basmati rice or 2 x 250g microwave pouches (to serve with the chickpea curry)

STORECUPBOARD
- ○ Sea salt and black pepper
- ○ Sunflower oil
- ○ Olive oil
- ○ Curry powder
- ○ Paprika
- ○ Sweet smoked paprika
- ○ Cajun seasoning
- ○ American mustard
- ○ Dijon mustard
- ○ Chilli sauce (optional)
- ○ Tomato ketchup
- ○ Worcestershire sauce
- ○ Soft light brown sugar
- ○ Runny honey
- ○ Vegetable stock cubes
- ○ Jalapeños (optional)
- ○ Cider vinegar
- ○ Mango chutney (optional)

* Buy frozen if you prefer

MONDAY

Chickpea Peanut Butter Curry (p. 62)

TUESDAY

15-minute Fish Tacos (p. 140)

WEDNESDAY

No-stir Chorizo Risotto (p. 118)

THURSDAY

15-minute Florentine Chicken Pasta (p. 76)

FRIDAY

Sloppy Joe Sandwiches (p. 170)
Cheesy Corn (p. 172)

SATURDAY

Crunchy Cutlets (p. 104)
Warm Waldorf Potatoes (p. 106)

WEEKEND BREAKFAST

Full English Bake (p. 40)

TREATS

Salted Pretzel Fudge (p. 200)

MONDAY

Cauliflower Cheese Soup *(p. 54)*
Parmesan Croutons *(p. 57)*

TUESDAY

Pot Pie in a Pinch
(p. 102)

WEDNESDAY

Fully Loaded Fish Naan *(p. 130)*

THURSDAY

Cheat's Tortilla Pizzas *(p. 96)*
Cheeky Chopped Salad *(p. 106)*

FRIDAY

Friday Night Fried Rice
(p. 122)

SATURDAY

20-minute Beef Stroganoff Pasta
(p. 88)

WEEKEND BREAKFAST

Sky-high Blueberry Pancakes
(p. 42)

TREATS

Biscuit Tin Tiffin
(p. 195)

WEEK 4: SHOPPING LIST

FRUIT & VEG

- 4 onions*
- 1 small red onion
- 3 spring onions
- 7 garlic cloves*
- 3 carrots
- 3 celery sticks
- 3 peppers ← *whichever colour you prefer*
- 250g chestnut mushrooms
- 1 cauliflower (about 800g)
- 2 cucumbers
- 2 lemons (for lemon juice!)
- 360g tomatoes (about 6 large)
- 25g fresh parsley
- 300g blueberries
- Toppings for your 'pizzas' (we like slices of mushrooms/peppers)

MEAT/FISH

- 650g skinless, boneless chicken breasts
- 500g beef mince
- 400g frozen large raw peeled prawns
- 4 cod fillets or other white fish (about 500g in total – use frozen and defrost if you prefer)
- Toppings for your 'pizzas' (we like slices of pepperoni/ham)

FRIDGE/FREEZER

- 700ml whole milk
- 400ml milk of your choice
- 150g unsalted butter
- 150g mature Cheddar cheese
- 150g grated mozzarella or Cheddar cheese
- 200g garlic and herb cream cheese
- 25g Parmesan cheese
- 200ml natural yoghurt
- Greek yoghurt (optional)
- 320g ready-rolled puff pastry (from the fridge, or from the freezer and then defrosted is fine)
- 150g frozen peas
- 450g mixed frozen vegetables

EVERYTHING ELSE

- 200ml passata
- 2 x 250g microwave rice pouches
- 300g dried tagliatelle
- 4 large soft tortillas
- 4 naan breads
- 50g Brazil nuts
- 300g stale bread ← *whichever type you have is fine*
- 400g biscuits ← *leftovers from the cupboard are fine!*
- 350g milk chocolate
- 200g plain chocolate (minimum 55–70% cocoa solids)
- Flaked almonds (optional, to serve with the pancakes)
- 6 eggs

STORECUPBOARD

- Sea salt and black pepper
- Sunflower oil
- Olive oil
- Dried oregano
- Garlic granules
- Ground cumin
- Garam masala
- Chinese 5-spice
- Dried thyme
- Chicken stock cubes
- Vegetable stock cubes
- Beef stock cubes
- Worcestershire sauce
- Dijon mustard
- Dark soy sauce
- Oyster sauce
- Wholegrain mustard
- Mint sauce (the vinegary type, not mint jelly)
- Golden syrup
- Baking power
- Honey (optional, to serve with the pancakes)
- Caster sugar
- Plain flour
- Self-raising flour

* Buy frozen if you prefer

WEEK 5: SHOPPING LIST

FRUIT & VEG
- 1 onion*
- ½ red onion
- 12 spring onions
- 2 garlic cloves*
- 2 courgettes
- 3 red peppers
- 2 tomatoes (optional)
- 350g butternut squash (or frozen)
- 500g cauliflower (or one whole head)
- 1 cucumber
- 7 limes
- 1 ripe mango
- 400g pineapple (I buy a tub of ready-chopped from the supermarket)
- lettuce leaves (for your burgers)
- 5g fresh mint

MEAT/FISH
- 200g smoked bacon lardons
- 600g mini chicken fillets
- 500g lamb mince
- 4 skinless, boneless chicken breasts (about 600g in total)
- 8 streaky bacon rashers
- 120g ham, about 8 thin slices
- 4 salmon fillets (about 500g in total)

FRIDGE/FREEZER
- 900ml whole milk
- 100g Greek yoghurt
- 200g garlic and herb cream cheese
- 470g mature Cheddar cheese
- 4 slices of Cheddar cheese
- 200g fresh tomato salsa (from the supermarket dips aisle)
- 200g frozen peas

EVERYTHING ELSE
- 1 x 400g tin chopped tomatoes
- 2 x 200g tin sweetcorn
- 1 x 400g tin black beans

- 300g basmati rice (or 2 x 250g microwave pouches)
- 240g couscous
- 900g long-life ready-made gnocchi
- 300g dried macaroni pasta
- 4 small tortilla wraps
- 4 burger buns
- 4 croissants
- 25g flaked almonds
- 50g roasted peanuts
- 50g crunchy peanut butter
- 300g sugar-free smooth peanut butter
- 30g dried breadcrumbs ← *I like Panko*
- 1 egg

STORECUPBOARD
- Sea salt and black pepper
- Sunflower oil
- Olive oil
- Garlic granules
- Curry powder
- Ras el hanout spice mix
- Cajun seasoning
- Sweet smoked paprika
- Soy sauce
- Runny honey
- Vegetable stock cubes
- Soft dark brown sugar
- Tomato ketchup
- Dijon mustard
- Wholegrain mustard
- Sweet chilli sauce
- Jalapeños (from a jar)
- Cornflour
- Tomato purée
- Jam
- Caster sugar

* Buy frozen if you prefer

MONDAY

Cauli Mac & Cheese
(p. 74)

TUESDAY

Crispy Gnocchi with Bacon
(p. 86)

WEDNESDAY

Sticky Peanut Strips
(p. 186)
Crunchy Peanut Salad *(p. 183)*

THURSDAY

Lazy Lamb Tagine
(p. 116)

FRIDAY

Barbecue Chicken Burgers *(p. 174)*
Cowboy Caviar *(p. 173)*

SATURDAY

Crispy Salmon with Pineapple Salsa
(p. 164)

WEEKEND BREAKFAST

Savoury Stuffed Croissants
(p. 36)

TREATS

Peanut Butter & Jelly Cookies
(p. 202)

MONDAY

Lentil Linguine *(p. 50)*

TUESDAY

Sticky Gammon Steaks *(p. 126)*
Quick Colcannon *(p. 107)*

WEDNESDAY

Coconut Curried Salmon *(p. 100)*

THURSDAY

Moroccan-style Chicken with Couscous *(p. 150)*

FRIDAY

Parmesan Crusted Cod *(p. 162)*
Balsamic Potatoes *(p. 158)*

SATURDAY

One-pan Lasagne *(p. 80)*

WEEKEND BREAKFAST

Peach Cobbler Baked Oats *(p. 34)*

TREATS

Ivy's Cheese Scones *(p. 190)*

WEEK 6: SHOPPING LIST

FRUIT & VEG
- 2 onions*
- 9 garlic cloves*
- 3 tsp fresh ginger*
- 750g new potatoes
- 1kg white potatoes (such as Maris Piper or King Edward)
- 300g Savoy cabbage
- 3 peppers   *whichever colour you prefer*
- 6 large carrots
- 2 lemons
- 2 limes
- 3 celery sticks
- 500g green beans
- Flat leaf parsley (optional)

MEAT/FISH
- 4 skinless, boneless chicken breasts (about 600g in total)
- 500g beef mince (10 per cent fat content)
- 4 gammon steaks (about 800g in total)
- 4 cod fillets (about 500g in total)
- 4 salmon fillets (about 500g in total)

FRIDGE/FREEZER
- 110g butter
- 300ml whole milk
- 200ml milk of your choice
- 200g mature Cheddar cheese
- 150g grated mozzarella cheese
- 30g Parmesan cheese
- 200g frozen peas

EVERYTHING ELSE
- 1 x 400g tin coconut milk
- 680g passata (choose one with garlic and herbs included, if possible)
- 1 x 411g tin peaches slices in juice
- 75g walnuts
- 200g dried red lentils
- 2 x 400g tins chopped tomatoes

* Buy frozen if you prefer

- 300g dried linguine
- 250g dried lasagne sheets
- 240g couscous
- 2 x 250g microwave rice pouches (or regular rice if you have time)
- 160g rolled oats
- 60g dried breadcrumbs   *I like Panko*
- 75g dried apricots
- 3 tbsp Thai red curry paste
- 5 eggs

STORECUPBOARD
- Sea salt and black pepper
- Sunflower oil
- Olive oil
- Ground cumin
- Dried oregano
- Ground turmeric
- Paprika
- Chinese 5-spice
- Ground cinnamon
- Wholegrain mustard
- Dijon mustard
- English mustard powder
- Vegetable stock cubes
- Beef stock cubes
- Soy sauce
- Tomato purée
- Balsamic vinegar
- Runny honey
- Marmalade
- Baking powder
- Plain flour
- Soft dark brown sugar
- Soft light brown sugar

WEEK 7: SHOPPING LIST

FRUIT & VEG
- 3 onions*
- 1 red onion
- 2 garlic cloves*
- 750g white potatoes (such as Maris Piper or King Edward)
- 4 spring onions
- 1 cauliflower (about 500g)
- 1 broccoli (about 225g)
- 3 carrots
- 150g baby spinach leaves
- 200g cherry tomatoes
- 2 tomatoes (optional – for your croissants, use some extra cherry tomatoes if you prefer)
- 4 peppers (your colour of choice – but include at least 1 red)
- 1½ cucumbers
- 1 lettuce (I like romaine)
- 3 avocados
- 30g fresh mint
- 7 limes

MEAT/FISH
- 90g prosciutto (about 6 thin slices)
- 4 skinless, boneless chicken breasts (about 600g in total)
- 400g sausages
- 450g sirloin steak
- 200g smoked bacon lardons
- 500g skinless salmon fillets, bones removed

FRIDGE/FREEZER
- 150g unsalted butter
- 500ml whole milk
- 400g natural yoghurt
- Sour cream (to serve with fajitas or just use some extra yoghurt from the pot)
- 230g mature Cheddar cheese (plus extra to serve with the fajitas)
- 450g halloumi

- 75g Parmesan cheese
- 60g mayonnaise
- 320g ready-rolled puff pastry

EVERYTHING ELSE
- 1 x 400g tin black beans
- 2 x 400g tins chopped tomatoes
- 2 x 250g microwave rice pouches (or regular rice if you prefer)
- 300g dried spaghetti
- 200g couscous
- 100g white chocolate
- 200g milk chocolate
- 200g plain chocolate (minimum 55–70% cocoa solids)
- 150g mini marshmallows
- 120g toffee popcorn
- 4 mini naan breads
- 8 small tortilla wraps
- 1 egg

STORECUPBOARD
- Sea salt and black pepper
- Sunflower oil
- Olive oil
- Paprika
- Garlic granules
- Tikka spice mix
- Fennel seeds
- Ground cumin
- Garam masala
- Cayenne pepper
- Wholegrain mustard
- Cornflour
- Vegetable stock cubes
- Mint sauce (the vinegary type, not mint jelly)
- Mango chutney
- Chilli sauce
- Sweet chilli sauce
- Golden syrup
- Tomato purée

* Buy frozen if you prefer

MONDAY

Hot Halloumi with Crunchy Couscous *(p. 66)*

TUESDAY

Chicken Tikka-style Naan Burgers *(p. 184)*
Spiced Cauliflower Salad *(p. 182)*

WEDNESDAY

Sausage Spaghetti with Spinach *(p. 90)*

THURSDAY

Sheet-pan Steak Fajitas *(p. 110)*
Minty Smashed Avocados *(p. 107)*

FRIDAY

Salmon Bite Bowls *(p. 138)*

SATURDAY

Broccoli & Bacon Bake *(p. 132)*

WEEKEND BREAKFAST

Cheese & Ham Puffs *(p. 46)*

TREATS

Toffee Popcorn Rocky Road *(p. 206)*

MONDAY

Smoky Halloumi Bean Bake
(p. 60)

TUESDAY

Greek Chicken Bowls
(p. 146)

WEDNESDAY

Zesty Lamb Pittas *(p. 168)*
Roasted Aubergine Salad *(p. 172)*

THURSDAY

Pea Pesto Pasta with Pancetta *(p. 70)*

FRIDAY

Sticky Ginger Pork
(p. 108)

SATURDAY

Fish Pie in a Flash
(p. 128)
Minty Greens *(p. 129)*

WEEKEND BREAKFAST

Bacon, Egg & Cheese Muffins
(p. 38)

TREATS

Chocolate Brownie Cookies *(p. 194)*

WEEK 8: SHOPPING LIST

FRUIT & VEG

- ○ 1 onion*
- ○ 1 red onion
- ○ 6 garlic cloves*
- ○ 3 tsp ginger purée*
- ○ 500g butternut squash*
- ○ 200g sugar snap peas
- ○ 1 lettuce (whichever type you fancy)
- ○ 1½ cucumbers
- ○ 2 large aubergines
- ○ 3 lemons
- ○ 200g long stem broccoli
- ○ 200g cherry tomatoes
- ○ 1 Savoy cabbage
- ○ 10g fresh flat leaf parsley
- ○ 5g fresh mint

MEAT/FISH

- ○ 500g pork mince
- ○ 500g lean lamb mince
- ○ 500g chicken mince
- ○ 8 bacon rashers
- ○ 200g smoked bacon lardons
- ○ 640g fish pie mix*
- ○ 150g cooked prawns*

FRIDGE/FREEZER

- ○ 100g salted butter
- ○ 150g unsalted butter
- ○ 4 slices smoked cheese
- ○ 450g halloumi
- ○ 40g Parmesan cheese
- ○ 200g feta cheese
- ○ 400g Greek yoghurt
- ○ 200g hummus
- ○ 135g filo pastry, (about 3–4 sheets)
- ○ 650g frozen peas
- ○ 500ml whole milk, plus an extra 2 tbsp

EVERYTHING ELSE

- ○ 2 x 400g tins chopped tomatoes
- ○ 2 x 400g tins mixed beans
- ○ 100g white chocolate chips
- ○ 100g plain chocolate chips
- ○ 4 English muffins
- ○ 300g dried pasta
- ○ 4 x 250g microwave rice pouches (or regular rice if you have time)
- ○ 40g dried breadcrumbs ← *I like Panko*
- ○ Crusty bread (to serve with halloumi bake)
- ○ 4 large pitta breads
- ○ 50g pine nuts
- ○ 100g black olives (optional)
- ○ 10 eggs

STORECUPBOARD

- ○ Sea salt and black pepper
- ○ Sunflower oil
- ○ Olive oil
- ○ Cornflour
- ○ Soy sauce
- ○ Runny honey
- ○ Oyster sauce
- ○ White wine vinegar
- ○ Chinese 5-spice
- ○ Ground cumin
- ○ Ground coriander
- ○ Dried oregano
- ○ Garlic granules
- ○ Sweet smoked paprika
- ○ Mint sauce (the vinegary type, not mint jelly)
- ○ Tomato purée
- ○ Cocoa powder
- ○ Baking powder
- ○ Caster sugar
- ○ Soft dark brown sugar
- ○ Plain flour

* Buy frozen if you prefer

WEEK 9: SHOPPING LIST

FRUIT & VEG

- ○ 3 onions*
- ○ 9 garlic cloves*
- ○ 750g new potatoes
- ○ 750g white potatoes (such as Maris Piper or King Edward)
- ○ 1 red pepper
- ○ 2 green peppers
- ○ 3 celery sticks
- ○ 3 large courgettes
- ○ 300g green beans (or use frozen as you're buying anyway)
- ○ 1 large iceberg lettuce
- ○ lettuce leaves (for the burgers)
- ○ 150g cherry tomatoes
- ○ 4 eating apples
- ○ 7 lemons
- ○ 150g raspberries

MEAT/FISH

- ○ 400g pork sausages (about 6 in total)
- ○ 500g skinless, boneless chicken breasts
- ○ 500g lean beef mince
- ○ 300g smoked bacon lardons
- ○ 4 salmon fillets (about 500g in total)

FRIDGE/FREEZER

- ○ 160ml milk of your choice
- ○ 250ml whole milk
- ○ 160g Greek yoghurt
- ○ 150g unsalted butter
- ○ 200g feta cheese
- ○ 100g grated mozzarella cheese
- ○ 4 cheese slices
- ○ 180g mayonnaise
- ○ 200ml crème fraîche
- ○ 150g frozen peas
- ○ 200g frozen green beans

EVERYTHING ELSE

- ○ 1 x 400g tin chopped tomatoes
- ○ 3 x 325g tins sweetcorn*
- ○ 300g dried spaghetti
- ○ 240g couscous
- ○ 200g long-grain rice
- ○ 160g rolled oats
- ○ 75g dried breadcrumbs
- ○ 40g raisins *← I like Panko*
- ○ 50g pine nuts (optional)
- ○ 2 gherkins (optional)
- ○ 4 burger buns (such as brioche)
- ○ 4 part-baked bread rolls
- ○ 7 eggs

STORECUPBOARD

- ○ Sea salt and black pepper
- ○ Sunflower oil
- ○ Olive oil
- ○ Garlic granules
- ○ Onion powder
- ○ Dried oregano
- ○ Cajun or fajita seasoning
- ○ Sweet smoked paprika
- ○ Mixed spice
- ○ Vegetable stock cubes
- ○ Chicken stock cubes
- ○ Balsamic vinegar
- ○ American mustard
- ○ Green pesto
- ○ Tomato ketchup
- ○ Tomato purée
- ○ Runny honey
- ○ Baking powder
- ○ Caster sugar
- ○ Plain flour
- ○ Self-raising flour

* Buy frozen if you prefer

MONDAY
Garlic Bread Spaghetti *(p. 78)*

TUESDAY
Bacon & Corn Chowder *(p. 144)*

WEDNESDAY
Garlic Feta Loaded Salmon *(p. 114)*

THURSDAY
Loaded Sausage Subs *(p. 178)*
Pesto Potato Salad *(p. 182)*

FRIDAY
One-pot Cajun-style Chicken & Rice *(p. 134)*

SATURDAY
Speedy Smash Burgers *(p. 176)*
Wedge Salad *(p. 173)*

WEEKEND BREAKFAST
Apple Pie Baked Oats *(p. 35)*

TREATS
Lemon & Raspberry Muffins *(p. 204)*

MONDAY

Get Well Soon Soup *(p. 52)*
Double Cheese Garlic
Bread *(p. 56)*

TUESDAY

Sticky Turkey Tacos
(p. 156)
Zesty Lime Slaw *(p. 159)*

WEDNESDAY

Hotpot in a Hurry
(p. 124)

THURSDAY

Hawaiian-style Pork
(p. 112)

FRIDAY

**Storecupboard
Spaghetti** *(p. 72)*

SATURDAY

**Sausage & Mash
with a Secret** *(p. 120)*

WEEKEND BREAKFAST

**Sweetcorn Feta
Fritters** *(p. 30)*

TREATS

**Strawberry
Shortcakes** *(p. 198)*

WEEK 10: SHOPPING LIST

FRUIT & VEG
- 5 onions*
- 9 garlic cloves*
- 1.75kg white potatoes (such as Maris Piper or King Edward)
- 500g parsnips
- 10 spring onions
- 5 carrots
- 3 celery sticks
- 2 leeks
- 1 green pepper
- 200g baby sweetcorn
- 75g strawberries (about 6)
- 1 avocado
- ¼ white cabbage (use the rest for lunchtime salads)
- 2 green apples
- 4 limes
- Flat-leaf parsley (optional)

MEAT/FISH
- 500g pork tenderloin
- 500g turkey mince
- 500g beef mince
- 8 pork sausages (about 450g)

FRIDGE/FREEZER
- 300ml milk of your choice
- 175g salted butter
- 40g unsalted butter
- 125ml double cream
- 20g Parmesan cheese
- 150g feta cheese
- 100g ready-grated mozzarella cheese
- 200g tub of fresh salsa
- 100g Greek yoghurt
- 150ml soured cream
- 75g mayonnaise

EVERYTHING ELSE
- 2 x 325g cans sweetcorn
- 1 x 400g tin black beans
- 250g dried red lentils

- 350g dried spaghetti
- 680g passata (one with garlic and herbs is even better if you have it)
- 2 x 250g microwave rice pouches (or regular rice if you have time)
- 2 part-baked baguettes
- 2 x 145g tins tuna
- 100g pitted olives
- 1 x 260g tin pineapple chunks in juice
- 8 small tortilla wraps
- 7 eggs

STORECUPBOARD
- Sea salt and black pepper
- Sunflower oil
- Olive oil
- Garlic granules
- Onion powder
- Paprika
- Ground turmeric
- Ground ginger
- Dried parsley
- Baking powder
- Vanilla extract
- Jam
- Balsamic vinegar
- Dried mixed Italian herbs
- Dried thyme
- Dried oregano
- Cornflour
- Ground ginger
- Sweet smoked paprika
- Runny honey
- Worcestershire sauce
- Ground cumin
- Paprika
- Vegetable stock cubes
- Beef stock cubes
- Tomato purée
- White wine vinegar
- Caster sugar
- Icing sugar
- Dark soft brown sugar
- Light soft brown sugar
- Plain flour

Buy frozen if you prefer

WEEKEND BREAKFASTS

SWEETCORN FETA FRITTERS

At this point, I feel the need to say, I am not the sort of person who ordinarily would have the energy or inclination to stand over a frying pan tending to fritters on a weekend morning. In this case, however, I'm willing to make an exception; these fritters are so easy to make, mostly from storecupboard ingredients, and are ready in about 20 minutes, including frying time. Even better, they are always a sure winner.

1. **Preheat the oven to the lowest setting to keep the fritters warm when cooked.**

2. **In a large mixing bowl, mix the flour, garlic granules, paprika and baking powder. Season with salt and pepper. Add the eggs and about half of the milk and mix until smooth, then add the rest of the milk and mix again until completely smooth.**

3. **Stir in the sweetcorn, onions and feta until combined.**

4. **Heat the oil in a large frying pan over a medium heat.**

5. **Dollop serving spoons full of the batter into the hot frying pan (hopefully you can fit in four at a time) and cook for about 4 minutes. When the bottoms start to turn golden, flip the fritters over and cook for the same length of time on the other side.**

6. **When the first lot of fritters are cooked, remove them from the pan with a spatula to an ovenproof dish, lined with kitchen paper, and keep them warm in the oven. Fry the next lot of fritters as before, so you end up with 8 in total. Keep them warm in the oven too.**

7. **If you are serving the fritters with a poached or fried egg, cook them now. Put two fritters on each place, dollop on a spoonful of salsa and finish with an egg on top.**

SERVES 4

2 tbsp sunflower oil
200g plain flour
1 tsp garlic granules
1 tsp paprika
1 tsp baking powder
2 eggs
150ml milk of your choice
2 x 325g cans sweetcorn, drained
4 spring onions, finely chopped
150g feta cheese, crumbled
sea salt and freshly ground
    black pepper

To serve:
4 poached or fried eggs (optional)
200g tub of fresh salsa

THRIFTY TIP

Substitute other vegetables for the sweetcorn if you have some to use up – broccoli works well. Just boil it until tender first, then leave to cool before adding to the fritter mixture. You can also swap the feta for whatever cheese you have available.

KIDS TIP

These made brilliant finger food for very young children. Just omit the salt, paprika and feta (as it's high in salt).

VERY BERRY BAKED OATS

When baked in this recipe, the berries turn into delicious little jammy pockets, waiting to be found as you dig into the oats. Ease yourself into the day by serving these with an extra drizzle of honey on top.

1. Preheat the oven to 180°C fan/200°C/Gas Mark 6.

2. Mix the berries, oats, eggs, milk, honey, baking powder and cinnamon in a large mixing bowl until combined. Spoon the mixture into 4 large ovenproof ramekins, about 10cm diameter.

3. Sprinkle the flaked almonds evenly over the top of each one.

4. Bake for 20–25 minutes, or until risen slightly and lightly golden. I like mine slightly gooey in the middle, but you can cook them for longer if you prefer a cakey texture. Leave to cool slightly and serve in the ramekins or turn out if preferred or serving to young children.

SERVES 4

260g mixed berries (blueberries and raspberries work well)
160g rolled oats
4 eggs
160ml milk of your choice
6 tsp runny honey
1 tsp baking powder
1 tsp ground cinnamon
25g flaked almonds

THRIFTY TIP

Frozen berries work brilliantly here and are often cheaper than fresh. You may need to cook them for slightly longer to properly heat them through.

PEACH COBBLER BAKED OATS

Modern shoppers seem to have forgotten tinned fruit, with good reason in some cases, but here the humble tinned peach is turned into something altogether more exciting. I bake these fruit oat cobblers in individual ramekins so that they cook more quickly, but they can also be made in a single large dish – you'll just need to cook it for slightly longer, about 30–40 minutes, depending on the size of the dish.

SERVES 4

1 x 411g tin peach slices in juice, drained (**250g** drained weight) and cut into small 1cm chunks
160g rolled oats
4 eggs
200ml milk of your choice
4 tsp runny honey
1 tsp baking powder
2 tsp ground cinnamon
2 tsp soft light brown sugar

1.   Preheat the oven to 180°C fan/200°C/Gas Mark 6.

2.   Mix the peaches, oats, eggs, milk, honey, baking powder and cinnamon in a large mixing bowl until combined. Spoon the mixture into 4 large ovenproof ramekins, about 10cm diameter.

3.   Sprinkle the brown sugar evenly over the top of each one.

4.   Bake for 20 minutes, or until risen slightly and lightly golden. I like mine slightly gooey in the middle, but you can cook them for longer if you prefer a cakey texture. Leave to cool slightly and serve in the ramekins or turn out if preferred or serving to young children.

BAKED OATS

• Use regular rolled porridge oats, rather than jumbo oats which won't soften enough in the cooking time.

• This is a great way to use up fruit that's past its best.

APPLE PIE BAKED OATS

Apple pie for breakfast? Now we're talking. Okay, it's not actual apple pie, but these baked oats remind me of the flavour, while also making a nutritious and filling breakfast. I like to serve them with a dollop of Greek yoghurt on top and a little extra honey.

1. **Preheat the oven to 180°C fan/200°C/Gas Mark 6.**

2. **Mix the apples, oats, eggs, milk, raisins, honey, baking powder and mixed spice in a large mixing bowl until combined. Spoon the mixture into 4 large ovenproof ramekins, about 10cm diameter.**

3. **Bake for 20–25 minutes, or until risen slightly and lightly golden. I like mine slightly gooey in the middle, but you can cook them for longer if you prefer a cakey texture. Leave to cool slightly and serve in the ramekins or turn out if preferred or serving to young children.**

SERVES 4

4 eating apples, grated, no need to peel
160g rolled oats
4 eggs
160ml milk of your choice
40g raisins
6 tsp runny honey
1 tsp baking powder
2 tsp mixed spice

BATCH COOKING BAKED OATS

You could make a double batch of any of the baked oat recipes and freeze. Once cooked, allow to cool, then wrap well and freeze in the ramekins for up to 1 month. (You can also turn them out of the cooking dish before freezing – you'll need to wait until cool, then run a knife carefully around the inside.) To serve, defrost overnight in the fridge and reheat in the microwave for about 2 minutes or until heated through. The reheating time will depend on the size of dish you use, and the power of your microwave. Also, bear in mind that you will need to cook the oats initially in microwave-safe ramekins if you do this.

SAVOURY STUFFED CROISSANTS

A taste of Paris on a Saturday morning? Don't mind if I do... These filled croissants take just a couple of minutes to put together and, if you have children, it's a simple kitchen task to let them help with – low risk for a very tasty result. I also find kids are much more likely to eat something that they've helped to make. Use a strong-tasting cheese to counter the sweetness of the buttery croissants.

1. Preheat the oven to 180°C fan/200°C/Gas Mark 6.

2. Slice the croissants through the middle to partly open them out. Spread each one with ½ teaspoon mustard, then fill with the ham, tomato slices and cheese.

3. Place on a baking sheet and bake for 10–15 minutes, until warmed through and the cheese has melted.

SERVES 4

4 croissants
2 tsp wholegrain mustard
120g ham, about 8 thin slices
2 tomatoes, cut into 1cm thick slices (optional)
120g mature Cheddar cheese, grated

THRIFTY TIP

To refresh croissants that are slightly past their best, sprinkle them with a little water before baking.

BACON, EGG & CHEESE MUFFINS

On those weekends when we have a house full of visitors, this is the breakfast I like to make. Presenting a platter piled with these filled muffins never fails to illicit a round of grateful oohs and aahs. Serve the muffins with a platter of fruit on the side, which everyone will ignore until they've had at least a second muffin.

1. Preheat the oven to 200°C fan/220°C/Gas Mark 7.

2. Spread the bacon out on a grill rack (the type where the fat can drip through onto the grill pan underneath) and place on the top shelf of the oven. Cook the bacon for 10 minutes, turning halfway, or until crisp.

3. After the bacon has been cooking for 5 minutes, put the muffin halves on a baking sheet in the oven. Warm the muffins for 5 minutes, turning once.

4. Meanwhile, cook the eggs. Melt the butter in a large, deep frying pan with a lid, over a low heat. Add the eggs and season with salt and pepper. Cook for 5 minutes, stirring until scrambled and lightly set. As they start to set, use a spatula or wooden spoon to divide into 4 piles of egg.

5. Place a slice of smoked cheese on top of each pile of egg. Put the lid on and cook for a couple of minutes on a very low heat. Turn off the heat and leave the lid on.

6. Remove the muffins from the oven, scoop a pile of cheesy egg onto one half of each muffin, then top with 2 rashers of bacon and the muffin lid. Serve warm.

SERVES 4

8 bacon rashers
4 English muffins, torn in half
50g salted butter
8 eggs, lightly beaten
4 slices smoked cheese
sea salt and freshly ground
　　black pepper

When you split the muffins, rip them in half with the help of a fork, rather than a knife. That way when you toast them, they have more of a crispy texture than when cut with a knife.

If you're multiplying this recipe to serve more than 4 people, the egg 'piles' will become less defined. That's fine, just scoop the eggs out of the pan with a spoon when slightly set and the cheese has melted.

Serve the muffins with ketchup, brown sauce and chilli sauce on the table.

FULL ENGLISH BAKE

A strong cup of tea and the smell of bacon cooking is surely one of life's great weekend joys? If, like me, you like the idea of a traditional English breakfast, but not the mess, here's my compromise. Be sure to shuffle everything about in the pan before breaking in the eggs, so that you get the perfect mouthful containing a little bit of everything when you tuck in. It goes without saying that hot buttered toast on the side is non-negotiable.

1. Preheat the oven to 200°C fan/220°C/Gas Mark 7.

2. In a large frying pan, heat the oil over a high heat and cook the sausages for 5 minutes, turning occasionally, until starting to brown all over.

3. Cut the sausages into big chunks – I use scissors to cut each one into 3 pieces in the pan.

4. Add the bacon to the pan and cook for 2–3 minutes, until starting to crisp.

5. Next, add the tomatoes and mushrooms and cook for a further 5 minutes, stirring occasionally, until the sausage chunks are cooked through, and the bacon is crisp.

6. Pour the contents of the pan into a shallow ovenproof dish (or use the same pan if it's ovenproof) and break in the eggs. Season with salt and pepper and pop the dish in the oven for 15 minutes, or until the eggs set.

SERVES 4

1 tsp sunflower oil
400g sausages of choice (about 6)
4 bacon rashers,
    each cut into 3 pieces
2 large tomatoes, quartered
150g chestnut mushrooms,
    cut into bite-sized pieces
6 large eggs
sea salt and freshly ground
    black pepper

For a vegetarian option, replace the bacon and sausages with meat-free alternatives.

You can use whichever sausages your family prefers (with herbs or plain) or even chicken.

SKY-HIGH BLUEBERRY PANCAKES

I have a confession... making pancakes is not entirely fuss free – I'm sorry, but how can I write a family cookbook without this failsafe weekend pancake recipe that we all need in our life? That said, these will be done in under 30 minutes, even with the resting time. Serve with Greek yoghurt, honey and sprinkled with flaked almonds.

MAKES 12

300g self-raising flour
50g caster sugar
4 tsp baking powder
½ tsp salt
400ml milk of your choice
1 egg
300g blueberries
6 tsp sunflower oil

1. **Put the flour, sugar, baking powder and salt in a mixing bowl and stir until combined.**

2. **In a jug, measure the milk and whisk in the egg.**

3. **Add about two-thirds of the milk mixture to the dry ingredients and whisk until smooth. Add the rest of the milk mixture and stir in the blueberries. Leave to sit, covered, for 10 minutes. Preheat the oven to the lowest setting to keep the pancakes warm when cooked.**

4. **While you're waiting, heat 1 teaspoon oil in a non-stick frying pan (or use two pans, if possible, to speed up the cooking time) over a medium heat.**

5. **Dollop a serving spoon full of the batter into the pan to make a pancake (I try to fit 2 pancakes in each pan at a time, depending on the size of the frying pan). When bubbles form all over the surface of the pancake, flip to cook the other side until set and lightly golden.**

6. **Transfer the pancakes to a serving dish in the oven to keep warm while you make the remaining pancakes – the batter makes about 12 in total, adding more oil when needed.**

For years, my weekend pancakes have been mediocre at best, until I discovered these top pancake tips:

• Leave the batter to rest before frying.

• Use 2 non-stick frying pans at once to cut the cooking time.

• Accept that they will never be perfectly round (unless you have the patience to cook one at a time, I do not) and embrace the imperfections.

EGG MUFFIN CUPS

These baked eggs were one of our favourite finger foods when my children were toddlers, and they still love them now. They are something like a mini quiche, without the crust, and you could cook them a little less if you like a runny yolk for breakfast. Serve with buttery toast, baked beans or even in a toasted English muffin.

1. Preheat the oven to 180°C fan/200°C/Gas Mark 6.

2. Generously grease 8 cups of a deep muffin tin (use a pastry brush or some kitchen roll and don't skimp on the oil as it will help you get the baked eggs out in one piece).

3. Line each of the cups with a slice of ham, so it forms a cup shape.

4. Share the cherry tomatoes between each ham-lined cup, followed by a little cheese. Season with salt and pepper, then break an egg into each one.

5. Bake for 10 minutes, or until the egg is cooked to your liking.

6. Carefully run a dinner knife around the edge of each muffin to loosen it from the tin, then remove. Alternatively, leave them in the tin for 7–8 minutes and then they should come away easily.

MAKES 8

sunflower oil, for greasing
120g ham, about 8 thin slices
100g cherry tomatoes
    (about 12), halved
80g mature Cheddar cheese, grated
8 eggs
sea salt and freshly ground
    black pepper

Make a double batch and serve as a protein-packed snack during the week.

You could swap the tomatoes for another vegetable if you prefer – leftover cooked vegetables or peas straight from the freezer work well.

CHEESE & HAM PUFFS

Crunchy, flaky pastry with golden melted cheese and crispy prosciutto – if these aren't the words weekend breakfast dreams are made of, I don't know what are. This recipe makes 6, because it suits the size of the puff pastry sheet; at least one or two should be used as a 'tester' for the chef. Just to be sure they are okay!

1. Preheat the oven to 200°C fan/220°C/Gas Mark 7.

2. Unroll the sheet of puff pastry and cut it in half lengthways, then slice into thirds horizontally, so you end up with 6 squares.

3. Lay a slice of prosciutto (or a slice and a half, depending on how many you have) diagonally across each square, from corner to corner. Add a slice or two of tomato and sprinkle a little cheese on top of each.

4. To shape each puff, pull the two corners without the filling over the top of the prosciutto, tomato and cheese to make a roll shape and use a little beaten egg to secure the edges together, if needed. Repeat to make 6 in total.

5. Place the puffs on a lined baking sheet and brush any uncovered pastry with the beaten egg. (You can sprinkle a little more cheese on top, if you fancy.) Bake for 13–15 minutes, until the pastry is golden and cooked through.

MAKES 6

320g ready-rolled puff pastry
90g prosciutto (about 6 thin slices)
2 tomatoes, cut into 1cm thick slices (optional)
80g mature Cheddar cheese, coarsely grated
1 egg, beaten

You can use chilled or frozen puff pastry. If frozen, let it defrost before rolling it out.

Line your baking sheet with baking paper. You can use the sheet that the raw pastry comes in as a shortcut.

MEAT-FREE MONDAYS

LENTIL LINGUINE

Lentils are affordable, nutritious, filling and keep for ages in the cupboard – although I know not everyone shares my lasting love affair with them. This recipe is a brilliant way to introduce lentils to your family in a non-scary way: they are hidden in the herb tomato sauce with added nuts, which gives it a meaty texture. I hope it converts you to the charms of the humble lentil.

1. Heat the oil in a large saucepan over a medium heat. Add the onion, garlic, celery and carrots and cook for 5 minutes, until the vegetables start to soften.

2. Add the lentils, chopped tomatoes, tomato purée and oregano, then season with plenty of salt and pepper. Fill one of the empty tomato tins with water and pour that in too. Turn the heat down slightly and give everything a good stir. Cover with the lid and simmer for about 20 minutes, until the lentils are soft and tender. Stir it occasionally to stop it sticking to the bottom of the pan. You may need to add a splash more water.

3. Add the chopped walnuts and balsamic vinegar to the lentil sauce and cook for a further 5 minutes.

4. Meanwhile, cook the pasta in a big pan of boiling salted water following the instructions on the pack – it usually takes about 11 minutes. Drain the pasta, add to the sauce and mix everything together to serve.

2 tsp olive oil
1 onion, peeled and chopped
3 garlic cloves, peeled and crushed
3 celery sticks, finely chopped
4 carrots, peeled and finely chopped
200g dried red lentils, rinsed
2 x 400g tins chopped tomatoes
3 tbsp tomato purée
2 tsp dried oregano
300g dried linguine
75g walnuts, chopped into
  small pieces
3 tbsp balsamic vinegar
sea salt and freshly ground
  black pepper

You can make a double batch of this sauce and freeze (before adding the pasta) to use another day.

I like to use linguine, but any pasta shape you have is good.

GET WELL SOON SOUP

This soup is what I make when we are feeling under the weather, when our hearts or stomachs need soothing. Simple, low effort and nourishing, the soup contains turmeric and ginger, which are said to help ease tummy ills, and they also make it deliciously fragrant and warming. All that said, don't save it only for off days. It's just as good when you are feeling on top form served with dripping garlic bread – a dinner tale of two halves.

1. In a large saucepan, heat the oil over a medium heat. Add the onion, carrots and celery and cook for 5 minutes, or until softened.

2. Add the turmeric and ground ginger and cook for a couple of minutes, stirring, until everything is coated in the spices.

3. Add the lentils and stock. Season with plenty of salt and pepper and bring to the boil.

4. Once boiling, turn the heat to low, cover with the lid and simmer for 15–20 minutes, or until the lentils are soft and starting to turn mushy. Using a hand-held blender, blend until smooth, then serve, sprinkling over the parsley, if using.

SERVES 4

2 tsp sunflower oil
1 onion, peeled and chopped
3 carrots, peeled and cut into
    1cm pieces
3 celery sticks, sliced
1 tsp ground turmeric
1 tsp ground ginger
250g dried red lentils, rinsed
1 litre vegetable stock
    (made with a stock cube is fine)
sea salt and freshly ground
    black pepper
flat-leaf parsley, finely chopped,
    to garnish (optional)

It's not vital to cut the vegetables small, but the smaller you cut them, the quicker they will cook. If you prefer to leave them chunky, no problem but they will take slightly longer to soften.

THRIFTY TIP

Lentils are such a nutritious, affordable ingredient – make a double batch of this soup or freeze any leftovers for future meals.

SERVE WITH
Double Cheese Garlic Bread on page 56.

**DOUBLE CHEESE
GARLIC BREAD**
p. 56

CAULIFLOWER CHEESE SOUP

This soup is embarrassingly easy to make, but don't tell anyone because it tastes incredibly decadent. Blending cauliflower in a soup magically takes it from a pale, slightly uninspiring vegetable to a bowl of smooth, velvety goodness. What could make it even better? Cheese of course – use a mature Cheddar for a burst of flavour. I've also added some Parmesan croutons as a topping for added crunch.

1. **Put the cauliflower, onion and vegetable stock in a large saucepan. Season with salt and pepper, bring to the boil and cook for 15 minutes, or until the cauliflower is very soft.**

2. **Remove the pan from the heat. Add the milk, cheese and mustard and stir through. Using a hand-held blender, blend everything together until the soup is smooth.**

3. **Return to the heat for 3–5 minutes, until heated through. (If you are serving to young children, you may not want to bother with this step as they will probably need it a little cooler.) Check the seasoning and serve.**

SERVES 4

1 cauliflower (about **800g**), leaves removed and cut into small florets
1 onion, peeled and chopped
750ml vegetable stock
400ml milk, whole milk preferably
150g mature Cheddar cheese, coarsely grated
1 tsp wholegrain mustard
sea salt and freshly ground black pepper

For a shortcut, make this soup with frozen onions and/or cauliflower.

This soup freezes brilliantly and is perfect to serve on a chilly evening when you need a treat.

THRIFTY TIP

This soup is perfect for using up any small pieces of cheese you have in the fridge. Any mixture of strongly flavoured cheese works well.

SERVE WITH
Parmesan Croutons on page 57.

PARMESAN
CROUTONS
p. 57

SIDES

SERVES 4

DOUBLE CHEESE GARLIC BREAD

This is a really easy way of making those great-value supermarket baguettes something special.

2 part-baked baguettes
125g salted butter
4 garlic cloves, peeled and crushed
1 tsp dried parsley
½ tsp sea salt
20g Parmesan cheese, finely grated
100g ready-grated mozzarella cheese

**Preheat the oven to
200°C fan/220°C/Gas Mark 7.**

Cut each baguette in half lengthways and lay
the 4 halves on a baking sheet.

In a small bowl, mix the butter (if it's straight
from the fridge, soften it in the microwave
for 30 seconds), garlic, parsley, salt
and Parmesan together.

Slather the garlic butter over the cut side of
each baguette and top with the mozzarella.
Bake for 15 minutes, or until golden
and crispy.

I tend to use bags of ready-grated mozzarella here as they are handy to keep in the fridge, are good value and ready to use. If you'd prefer to use buffalo mozzarella, that will work too, just drain and cut it into small pieces before sprinkling on the buttered bread.

If you have any fresh parsley or other herbs, they work well instead of dried.

PARMESAN CROUTONS

Scatter these croutons over the soup just before serving. They also work brilliantly on top of salads to make them less... salady!

300g stale bread of choice
(no need to remove the crusts)
4 tbsp olive oil
4 garlic cloves, peeled and crushed
1 tsp dried oregano
½ tsp sea salt
25g Parmesan cheese, finely grated

Preheat the grill to medium-high.

Cut the bread into small (or not so small, up to you) cubes and toss in a bowl with the other ingredients.

Tip onto a grill-safe baking sheet and grill for 3–5 minutes, or until crisp and lightly golden. Keep an eye on them as they can easily burn and will need to be turned and shuffled every minute or so. Serve on top of the soup. The croutons will keep in an airtight tin for up to 3 days.

The croutons are a perfect way to use up stale bread (it's better than using fresh in fact).

GREEN GOODNESS SALAD

As someone who, on the whole, is not a big fan of lettuce, I've spent a lot of time trying to make it a bit more inspiring. I find that drenching it in this delicious sticky dressing certainly helps. Use extra-virgin olive oil if you have it; if you don't, regular olive oil also works, but just won't be quite as flavourful.

1 head of lettuce (I like romaine or butterhead), chopped into small pieces
1 punnet of cress, trimmed
1 ripe avocado, peeled, stone removed, and cut into 2cm chunks
1 green pepper, deseeded and cut into 2cm chunks
6 spring onions, chopped

For the Dressing:
1 garlic clove, peeled and crushed
1 tsp wholegrain mustard
1 tsp runny honey
3 tbsp olive oil, preferably extra-virgin
3 tbsp cider vinegar
½ tsp sea salt

Make the dressing by whisking all the ingredients together until smooth.

Add the salad ingredients to a serving bowl and pour the dressing over just before serving, then toss well.

FOUR-CHEESE FRITTATA

For those who dream of eating a full cheeseboard for dinner each night, like me, here's my nod to you. You can use whatever cheese you have in the fridge for this recipe, as long as it's the same weight. A mixture of soft goat's cheese and hard mature Cheddar work well – just make sure you have at least one strong flavoured one in there and it will be cheesy enough.

1. Cook the potatoes in a large saucepan of boiling salted water for 10–15 minutes, until cooked through and tender.

2. Meanwhile, heat the oil in a large, deep frying pan, or sauté pan (that can be used under a grill), over a low heat. Add the onion and slowly cook for 10 minutes, stirring occasionally.

3. Heat the grill to medium.

4. Drain the potatoes and add to the onions with the peas (no need to defrost them first). Season with plenty of salt and pepper and stir everything well.

5. Turn the heat up on the hob to medium. Pour the eggs into the pan over the vegetables – there's no need to mix everything together.

6. Sprinkle the four cheeses on top and cook the frittata for 5–10 minutes, until the bottom is set, but the top is still slightly runny.

7. Carefully place the pan under the grill and cook for a further 5 minutes, until the top is cooked. Serve cut into slices.

SERVES 4

750g new potatoes, scrubbed and cut into 2cm cubes
3 tbsp olive oil
1 large onion, peeled and thinly sliced
200g frozen peas
8 eggs, lightly beaten
100g soft goat's cheese, cut into small chunks
100g mozzarella cheese, drained and torn into small chunks
25g Parmesan cheese, finely grated
50g mature Cheddar cheese, grated
sea salt and freshly ground black pepper

For non-cheese fans, this recipe will also work without the cheese. You may want to add another vegetable, such as courgettes or mushrooms, fried with the onions, for extra flavour.

Leftover frittata makes a brilliant lunch served cold the next day.

THRIFTY TIP

This is a handy way to use up leftover pieces of cheese.

SERVE WITH
Green Goodness Salad on page 57.

GREEN
GOODNESS
SALAD
p. 57

SMOKY HALLOUMI BEAN BAKE

Cans of mixed beans make a nutritious, affordable storecupboard standby; let's be honest though, they aren't always terribly inspiring. Here, they are made infinitely more enticing with a topping of crispy halloumi. Serve with crusty bread to dunk into the smoky sauce.

1. In a large, deep frying pan (use a pan with a lid that can go under the grill), heat the oil over a medium heat. Add the onion, garlic, butternut squash, cumin and smoked paprika and cook for 5 minutes, stirring occasionally, until the onion and squash start to soften.

2. Add the chopped tomatoes, mixed beans and tomato purée. Season with salt and pepper. Fill one of the empty tomato tins with water and add to the pan. Cover with the lid and cook the sauce over a medium–low heat for 15 minutes, or until the butternut squash is tender. Stir the sauce occasionally to make sure it's not sticking to the bottom of the pan.

3. Meanwhile, preheat the grill to high.

4. When the sauce is cooked and thickened, lay the halloumi slices on top and drizzle with a little more oil. Pop the pan under the grill for 5 minutes, or until the halloumi is golden. Serve with crusty bread.

SERVES 4

2 tsp olive oil, plus extra for drizzling
1 onion, peeled and chopped
2 garlic cloves, peeled and chopped
500g butternut squash, peeled, seeds removed and chopped into bite-size pieces
2 tsp ground cumin
2 tsp sweet smoked paprika
2 x 400g tins chopped tomatoes
2 x 400g tins mixed beans, drained
3 tbsp tomato purée
450g halloumi, cut into thin slices
sea salt and freshly ground black pepper
crusty bread, to serve

To save time, I use frozen peeled and chopped butternut squash – bags of ready-prepared veg are so handy to keep in the freezer. If using frozen it may take slightly longer to cook.

THRIFTY TIP

Replace the butternut squash with any other vegetables that you have to hand that need to be used up.

CHICKPEA PEANUT BUTTER CURRY

This curry is one of my favourite storecupboard meals; somehow the additions of coconut milk and peanut butter turn whatever veggies I have hanging around in the fridge (often an aubergine, let's be honest) into something else entirely – a warming, fragrant treat! Feel free to swap the medium curry paste for a milder or hotter one, depending on your preferences.

1. In a saucepan, heat the oil over a medium heat. Add the onion, garlic and aubergine and cook, stirring occasionally, for 5 minutes, until the vegetables start to soften.

2. Add the curry powder and paprika, give everything a good stir and cook for 3–5 minutes, until the spices smell delicious.

3. Add the coconut milk, chickpeas, peanut butter and salt. Turn the heat down slightly, cover with the lid, and simmer for 20 minutes, stirring occasionally, until cooked through.

4. Cook the rice according to the packet instructions.

5. Just before serving, remove the pan from the heat and stir in the spinach and let it wilt before piling it onto your rice. Serve with a spoonful of mango chutney on the side.

SERVES 4

1 tsp sunflower oil
1 onion, peeled and chopped
2 garlic cloves, peeled and chopped
1 aubergine, chopped into small cubes
6 tsp medium curry powder
1 tsp paprika
1 x 400ml tin coconut milk
2 x 400g tins chickpeas, drained and rinsed
100g peanut butter or your choice of nut butter
½ tsp sea salt
100g baby spinach leaves

To serve
300g basmati rice (or 2 x microwave pouches)
Mango chutney

This is a brilliant recipe to make a double portion of and freeze half. Just cook as per the recipe and, when cool, freeze for up to 3 months. Defrost fully and reheat until hot all the way through.

THRIFTY TIP

Swap the vegetables here for any ones you have in your fridge that need to be used up. Cauliflower or frozen peas would also work well.

CHUNKY TORTELLINI SOUP

Filled pasta often calls to me when I'm in the supermarket, promising a meal in minutes, but I find a pack is never quite substantial enough for dinner. Here, I make a quick soup with a pack of filled pasta and lots of added vegetables to bulk it out. Don't forget the Parmesan on top – it's the crowning glory.

1. **In a large saucepan, heat the oil over a medium heat. Add the onion, garlic, carrots and celery and cook for 5 minutes, until starting to soften.**

2. **Add the chopped tomatoes, tomato purée and stock. Season with salt and pepper, stir and cook for 10 minutes, until the carrot is almost cooked through.**

3. **Add the peas, tortellini and pesto, stir and cook for a further 5–10 minutes, until the tortellini are heated through.**

4. **Ladle the soup into bowls and serve topped with Parmesan and a drizzle of olive oil.**

SERVES 4

1 tsp olive oil, plus extra for drizzling
1 onion, peeled and chopped
3 garlic cloves, peeled and crushed
3 carrots, peeled and chopped
    into 1cm pieces
2 celery sticks, chopped
    into 1cm pieces
1 x 400g tin chopped tomatoes
2 tbsp tomato purée
600ml hot vegetable stock
    (made with a cube is fine)
150g frozen peas
300g fresh, ambient or
    frozen tortellini
4 tbsp pesto of choice
sea salt and freshly ground
    black pepper
75g Parmesan cheese,
    finely grated, to serve

You can use whichever filled pasta you like – spinach and ricotta works well or try a meaty one.

If you are cooking for 'vegetable haters', blend the soup at the end of the second step before adding the peas, tortellini and pesto.

THRIFTY TIP

Swap the vegetables for any in your fridge that need to be used up.

HOT HALLOUMI WITH CRUNCHY COUSCOUS

I am convinced that there's not a mood or an occasion that can't be improved by halloumi cheese. When I root about in the fridge and find a pack ready to be pan fried, it's always a happy dinner time. Here, it's crisp, golden and sticky, and paired with a really fresh and light couscous salad.

1. Put the couscous in a large mixing bowl, pour over the hot stock and cover (I just pop a plate on top). Leave to sit for 10 minutes.

2. Meanwhile, make the yoghurt dressing by mixing all the ingredients together, then set aside.

3. In a large frying pan, heat the olive oil over a medium-high heat. Add the halloumi and cook for 5–10 minutes, turning the cubes occasionally, until golden and crisp.

4. While the halloumi is cooking, chop the cucumber, red pepper, cherry tomatoes and spring onions into very small pieces.

5. When the couscous is ready and has absorbed the stock, fluff it up using a fork, then add the chopped vegetables, the mint, olive oil and lime juice. Season with salt and pepper.

6. Take the halloumi pan off the heat and add the sweet chilli sauce. Stir until the halloumi is coated all over.

7. Serve the couscous topped with the halloumi and the yoghurt dressing drizzled over.

SERVES 4

200g couscous
300ml hot vegetable stock
    (made with a stock cube is fine)
½ cucumber
1 red pepper
200g cherry tomatoes
4 spring onions
10g fresh mint, finely chopped
2 tbsp olive oil
1 lime, juiced
sea salt and freshly ground
    black pepper

For the Yoghurt Dressing:
150g natural yoghurt
1 lime, juiced and zested
10g fresh mint, finely chopped

For the Halloumi:
1 tbsp olive oil
450g halloumi, cut into cubes
2 tbsp sweet chilli sauce

If you're not a chilli fan, replace the sweet chilli sauce with runny honey.

Any leftovers can be served cold the next day, and make a perfect packed lunch.

PASTA PLEASE

PEA PESTO PASTA WITH PANCETTA

There are not many recipes that I'd bother with that require the use of three pans, but this is one of them. I'm willing to forgive this dish as it's still ready within about 12 minutes. The freshness of the pea pesto combined with the smoky bacon is a match made in heaven.

1. Cook the pasta in a big pan of boiling salted water following the instructions on the pack – it usually takes about 11 minutes. About 5 minutes before the pasta is ready, add the broccoli and cook until both are tender. (You are going to use some of the cooking water in your pesto, so don't drain prematurely.)

2. Meanwhile, put the pancetta in a small dry frying pan and cook over a medium-high heat, turning occasionally, for 5–10 minutes, until crisp and golden.

3. In a small pan, cook the peas in boiling salted water for 5 minutes, or until just cooked. Drain and return them to the hot pan.

4. Add the remaining pesto ingredients to the peas and blend with a hand-held blender. Add a ladleful or two of the hot pasta cooking water to the pan and blend again until you have a fairly smooth, creamy pesto.

5. Drain the pasta and broccoli and return it to the hot pan, add the pesto, half of the fried pancetta lardons and toss well until combined.

6. Serve with the remaining pancetta cubes scattered over the top.

SERVES 4

300g dried pasta
200g long-stem broccoli, cut into small pieces
200g pancetta or smoked bacon lardons

For the Pea Pesto:
350g frozen peas
2 garlic cloves, peeled
40g Parmesan cheese, finely grated
2 tbsp olive oil
1 lemon, juiced and zested
50g pine nuts
sea salt and freshly ground black pepper

STORECUPBOARD SPAGHETTI

This is the recipe that we all need in our life for days when we can't face a trip to the supermarket – it has saved me more times than I care to remember. When the idea of cooking a meal feels like a monumental task, let this dinner, made with storecupboard ingredients, revive you. Whatever chaos is going on around, putting this down on the table always feels like a total win.

350g dried spaghetti
680g passata (one with garlic
and herbs is even better
if you have it)
½ tsp garlic granules
½ tsp onion powder
2 tsp dried mixed Italian herbs
2 tbsp olive oil
750ml hot vegetable stock
100g pitted olives
2 x 145g tins tuna, drained
2 tbsp balsamic vinegar
sea salt and freshly ground
black pepper

1. **Put all the ingredients, apart from the olives, tuna and balsamic vinegar, into a large saucepan. (Yes, the pasta goes in like that, dry!)**

2. **Cover with the lid and cook over a medium-low heat for 13 minutes, stirring occasionally, or until the pasta is cooked through. Keep an eye on the pasta as it cooks as it will almost certainly start to stick a little to the bottom of the pan. Just give it a good stir and turn the heat to low if it does – the sauce needs to gently bubble, rather than boil.**

3. **When the pasta is cooked, stir in the olives, tuna and balsamic. Season with plenty of salt and pepper and serve.**

Pitted olives are always easier to eat if you have them available. If you only have olives with stones in, you'll need to remove them by hand first if you're serving this to children.

A few easy options to add:

• a sprinkling of dried chilli flakes.

• frozen vegetables (or any fresh vegetables that you have to hand): peas, spinach or broccoli from the freezer all work well. Add them 5 minutes before the pasta is cooked.

• a tin of cannellini beans or butter beans for extra protein.

• freshly grated Parmesan cheese sprinkled over the top before serving.

CAULI MAC & CHEESE

A bowl of pasta swimming in cheese sauce is always going to be a star supper. Sneak in a whole head of cauliflower, and I can almost convince myself that it's practically a health food. If you have cauliflower objectors, cut the pieces very small and cook them for a little longer – they'll almost disappear into the sauce.

1. Cook the macaroni in a large pan of boiling salted water for 5 minutes, then add the cauliflower florets and cook for a further 5–8 minutes, until both are cooked through.

2. Meanwhile, make the sauce. Warm the milk in a medium-sized saucepan over a low-medium heat.

3. In a mug or bowl, mix 4 tablespoons of the milk with the cornflour to make a smooth paste, then stir it into the warm milk in the pan. Reduce the heat to low and stir for about 5 minutes, until the sauce starts to thicken. Add the mustard, garlic granules and 300g of the Cheddar. Season with salt and pepper, then stir for another couple of minutes until the cheese melts.

4. Preheat the grill to high.

5. When cooked, drain the pasta and cauliflower (give it a good shake to remove any excess water as otherwise the sauce will be watery) and place in a shallow heatproof dish (one that can be used under the grill, or you can use a roasting tin or ovenproof pan), then pour the cheese sauce over. Sprinkle with the remaining Cheddar and the breadcrumbs and pop the dish under the grill for 3–5 minutes, until the top is crisp and golden.

SERVES 4

300g dried macaroni
500g cauliflower (about 1 whole head), leaves removed and cut into small florets
750ml whole milk
50g cornflour
2 tsp wholegrain mustard
2 tsp garlic granules
350g mature Cheddar cheese, grated
30g dried breadcrumbs, such as panko
sea salt and freshly ground black pepper

THRIFTY TIP

Use frozen cauliflower, if easier – it's often cheaper and makes a convenient alternative to fresh.

15-MINUTE FLORENTINE CHICKEN PASTA

Can this Tuscan-style pasta dish transport us to Italy, relaxing by a pool in the sunshine? Okay, that might be a stretch, but this speedy dinner does use some of my favourite pasta shortcuts. Pasta water is a gem of a secret ingredient. The starchy water from the pasta transforms a tub of cream cheese into a silky sauce. Using cream cheese flavoured with garlic and herbs is another short-cut trick to add flavour with zero effort – perfect for quick dinners that still impress.

1. **Cook the pasta in a big pan of boiling salted water following the instructions on the pack – it usually takes about 11 minutes.**

2. **Meanwhile, heat the oil in a separate large pan over a medium heat. Add the chicken, season with salt and pepper, and cook for 10 minutes, stirring occasionally to stop the chicken sticking to the bottom of the pan.**

3. **Turn off the heat under the pan of chicken and add the sun-dried tomatoes, spinach, cream cheese and a ladleful of the pasta cooking water to the pan. Stir until smooth, adding more pasta water if needed.**

4. **Drain the pasta and add to the sauce with the Parmesan. Toss well until combined and serve straight away, with the basil leaves sprinkled over.**

SERVES 4

250g dried pasta
1 tbsp oil from the jar of
   sun-dried tomatoes
600g skinless, boneless chicken
   breasts, cut into small chunks
150g sun-dried tomatoes in oil,
   chopped into small pieces
80g baby spinach leaves
250g garlic and herb cream cheese
100g Parmesan cheese, finely grated
sea salt and freshly ground
   black pepper
basil leaves, to finish

You could use leftover cooked chicken here instead of raw. Omit the oil and there's no need to pan fry the chicken first. Just add the cooked chicken to the cooked pasta with the rest of the ingredients.

GARLIC BREAD SPAGHETTI

Double carbs? Yes please. If you've never tried topping pasta with crunchy breadcrumbs, you are in for a treat. They add a crunchy texture and little explosion of flavour in every pasta swirl. You could use shop-bought breadcrumbs, such as panko, or make your own blitzing stale bread into coarse crumbs in a food processor.

1. Cook the spaghetti in a big pan of boiling salted water following the instructions on the pack – it usually takes about 11 minutes. Set a timer for 7 minutes.

2. To prepare the crispy breadcrumbs, in a frying pan, heat the oil over a medium heat. Add the breadcrumbs, garlic and salt and fry, stirring often, until golden and toasted, and they smell delicious. The crumbs can burn easily so keep an eye on them. Tip the breadcrumbs into a bowl and set aside.

3. When your pasta has been cooking for 7 minutes (or 4 minutes before it is due to be ready), add the peas and green beans and continue to cook until tender.

4. Drain the cooked pasta and vegetables and return them to the hot pan. Stir in the crème fraîche, pesto and lemon juice. Season with salt and pepper and toss everything together until combined and heated through. Serve sprinkled with the crispy crumbs.

SERVES 4

300g dried spaghetti
150g frozen peas
200g green beans (I use frozen)
200ml crème fraîche
3 tbsp green pesto
1 lemon, juiced
sea salt and freshly ground
    black pepper

For the Crispy Breadcrumbs:
2 tbsp olive oil (not extra virgin)
75g dried breadcrumbs (from a packet is fine)
3 garlic cloves, peeled and crushed
½ tsp sea salt

Ready-made garlic purée works particularly well here, as I find it melts into the breadcrumbs more readily than large chunks of garlic, and also saves time. Find it in jars or tubes.

You could also add cooked chicken, or another type of protein, to this dish.

THRIFTY TIP

Frozen green beans are a fantastic freezer standby. They are also often cheaper than fresh.

PASTA PLEASE

ONE-PAN LASAGNE

Telling you that this may be the best recipe in the entire book feels something like admitting to having a favourite child. Of course, there are never favourite children (well, for no longer than a day at least), but I do love my quick version of lasagne. I adore real lasagne but never have the patience or time to make it during the week. This shortcut version still packs in plenty of flavour and the bonus is that it's all made in one pan.

1. **In a large, deep frying pan (that can be used under the grill), heat the oil over a medium heat. Add the mince and cook for 5 minutes, stirring with a wooden spoon to break up the meat, until browned all over.**

2. **Add the garlic, onion, carrots and oregano. Season with salt and pepper and cook for a further 5 minutes, stirring occasionally.**

3. **Add the passata, tomato purée and stock, give everything a good stir, cover with the lid, and cook for 5 minutes.**

4. **Snap the lasagne sheets in half and press them standing upwards into the sauce. (They will look slightly awkward but will soften quickly.) Pop the lid back on and cook over a medium heat for a further 10 minutes, stirring occasionally as the pasta cooks to make sure the sheets don't stick together.**

5. **Meanwhile, heat the grill to high.**

6. **Remove the lid from the pan, give everything a good stir, scatter the mozzarella over the top and pop the pan under the grill for 5 minutes, until the top starts to turn golden.**

1 tbsp olive oil
500g beef mince,
     10 per cent fat content
3 garlic cloves, peeled and crushed
1 onion, peeled and finely chopped
2 carrots, peeled and
     chopped into very small pieces
2 tsp dried oregano
680g passata (choose one with
     garlic and herbs included,
     if possible)
3 tbsp tomato purée
500ml hot beef stock
     (made with a stock cube is fine)
250g dried lasagne sheets
150g grated mozzarella cheese
sea salt and freshly ground
     black pepper

I usually use a 10 per cent fat mince for this, which is a good balance of flavour without being too heavy; 5 per cent will also work but have a little less flavour, while 20 per cent fat mince may be a little greasy, but it's all personal preference.

Many supermarkets sell fresh or frozen bags of sofritto – a combination of finely chopped onions, celery and carrots. You can use it here to save yourself lots of chopping.

15-MINUTE 'BLT' PASTA

This pasta dish replicates the flavours of the BEST sandwich combo – I won't hear otherwise, thanks. I've replaced the lettuce (the 'L' in the traditional BLT) with spinach, which cooks almost instantly in the heat of the pasta. This pasta is also a winner of a side dish for barbecues or parties, and leftovers make a great lunchbox filler.

1. Cook the pasta in a big pan of boiling salted water following the instructions on the pack – it usually takes about 11 minutes.

2. Meanwhile, heat a large, dry frying pan over a medium-high heat and add the lardons. Cook for 8 minutes, turning regularly, or until crisp and golden, and the fat has rendered out of the bacon.

3. Add the tomatoes to the lardons and cook for a couple of minutes until just softened.

4. Drain the pasta and return it to the hot pan. Add the bacon and tomatoes (along with any fat from the bacon) to the pasta.

5. Stir in the spinach, crème fraîche, mustard and Parmesan. Season with salt and pepper. Stir well and allow the heat of the pasta to wilt the spinach and warm the sauce.

SERVES 4

300g dried pasta
200g smoked bacon lardons
300g cherry tomatoes, halved
80g baby spinach leaves
300ml crème fraîche
2 tsp wholegrain mustard
75g Parmesan cheese, finely grated
sea salt and freshly ground
     black pepper

Buy pre-washed spinach to save preparation time.

THRIFTY TIP

I use ready-cut cubes of bacon to save time – they also give a smoky flavour and crispy texture to the dish. Swap it for regular bacon, if cheaper, and snip it into small pieces using scissors.

ONE-POT LAMB ORZO

If you've never used orzo before, it's so worth finding some for this recipe (orzo is a small pasta shape that looks like a grain of rice). Here, it's cooked in one pan with the lamb and the result is a rich, meaty sauce with the plump pasta nestled in, a bit like a pasta risotto.

1. Heat a large saucepan over a high heat and add the lamb mince. (You shouldn't need any oil as lamb mince tends to have a high fat content.) Cook for 5 minutes, stirring occasionally with a wooden spoon to break up the mince, until the lamb is browned all over.

2. Add the cumin, oregano, garlic granules and red peppers. Give everything a good stir and cook for a further 5 minutes, stirring occasionally, until the peppers start to soften.

3. Add the tomato purée, orzo and stock. Season with plenty of salt and pepper, stir well and cover with the lid. Cook for 13–15 minutes over a low heat, stirring occasionally, until the orzo is just tender.

4. Turn off the heat under the pan, stir in the spinach (it will wilt and cook within a minute or two in the heat of the sauce) and squeeze over the lemon juice.

5. Serve the orzo and meat sauce with the feta crumbled over the top if you like – I always do.

SERVES 4

500g lamb mince
2 tsp ground cumin
2 tsp dried oregano
1 tsp garlic granules
2 red peppers, deseeded and cut into 2cm chunks
3 tbsp tomato purée
250g dried orzo
1 litre hot vegetable stock (made with a cube is fine)
100g baby spinach leaves
1 lemon, juiced
100g feta cheese, crumbled (optional)
sea salt and freshly ground black pepper

This also works well with other types of mince, like beef or veggie, if you prefer.

CRISPY GNOCCHI WITH BACON

Packets of long-life, ready-made gnocchi that live happily on supermarket shelves (I'm not talking about the ones in the chiller cabinet) are always worth keeping in your storecupboard. By some wizardry, they have a shelf life of months, if not years – poised and ready to be opened to provide carb comfort whenever it's needed. Here, we fry the little dumplings, rather than boiling, which makes a change from their usual soft texture.

1. Heat 1 tablespoon of the oil in a large, deep frying pan over a medium heat. Add half of the gnocchi and fry for 5–7 minutes, until golden and crispy.

2. Tip the gnocchi out of the pan and into a bowl. Repeat with the remaining oil and gnocchi – frying the gnocchi in two batches helps them to become evenly crispy. Set aside.

3. Turn the heat up to high and return the pan to the heat. Add the lardons and cook for 5 minutes, turning occasionally. Reduce the heat to medium, then add the courgettes and cook for a further 5 minutes.

4. Stir in the cream cheese, milk and peas, then season with plenty of black pepper. Let everything bubble away for 5 minutes, until the peas are cooked, and the cream cheese has melted into the sauce. Add the gnocchi back to the pan to warm through and turn to coat in the sauce. Taste and add salt, if needed; the bacon is quite salty so you probably won't.

SERVES 4

2 tbsp olive oil
900g long-life ready-made gnocchi
200g smoked bacon lardons
2 courgettes, cut into small chunks
200g garlic and herb cream cheese
150ml whole milk
200g frozen peas
sea salt and freshly ground
    black pepper

You can use chilled gnocchi here, if you prefer, but I find that the vacuum-packed, long-life ones work just as well here, if not better.

THRIFTY TIP

I use ready-cut cubes of bacon to save time – they also give a smoky flavour and crispy texture to the dish. Swap it for regular bacon, if cheaper, and snip it into small pieces using scissors.

20-MINUTE BEEF STROGANOFF PASTA

Traditional beef stroganoff is one of my favourite classic meals, but who can justify buying very expensive beef fillet for a quick weekday supper? Here, is my midweek take on the classic using beef mince and my favourite garlic and herb cream cheese shortcut. Don't forget the trick of adding a stock cube to the pasta cooking water for extra oomph.

1. Heat the oil in a large, deep frying pan over a high heat. Add the mince and cook for 10 minutes over a medium heat, stirring with a wooden spoon to break up the mince, until browned all over.

2. Meanwhile, cook the pasta in a big pan of boiling water (add the stock cubes to the water to flavour it.) Follow the instructions on the pasta pack – it usually takes about 11 minutes.

3. Add the onion and mushrooms to the mince and cook for 5 minutes, stirring often, until the onion has softened, and the mushrooms are cooked through.

4. Reduce the heat under the pan and add the cream cheese, Worcestershire sauce, half of the chopped parsley and a ladleful of the pasta cooking water to the mince mixture. Stir to make a smooth sauce.

5. Drain the pasta, add it to the sauce and toss well until combined. Serve with the remaining parsley sprinkled on top.

SERVES 4

2 tsp olive oil
500g beef mince
2 beef stock cubes
300g dried tagliatelle
1 onion, peeled and chopped
250g chestnut mushrooms, thinly sliced
200g garlic and herb cream cheese
2 tbsp Worcestershire sauce
25g fresh parsley, finely chopped

If your family aren't fans of mushrooms, you can substitute for another vegetable, such as green beans or broccoli, if you prefer.

SAUSAGE SPAGHETTI WITH SPINACH

Starting this recipe by giving the sausages 10 minutes alone in the pan gives the sauce a certain savoury edge. I promise, they are worth the wait. Use the best-quality sausages you can afford – you will be able to taste the difference. Even if fennel seeds are new to you, please do give them a try – they really take this dish to a new level and go so well with sausages. Just use them sparingly as they can be over-powering.

1. Put a large saucepan over a medium-high heat and squeeze the sausages out of their skins into the pan. Using a wooden spoon, break up the sausages and cook for 10 minutes, until browned. Move the sausages occasionally to stop it sticking to the bottom of the pan, but not too much or it will take longer to brown – the sausages should be in small pieces (a bit like mince) and golden in colour when ready.

2. Reduce the heat, add the onions and garlic and cook for a further 5 minutes, stirring often, until softened.

3. Next, add the chopped tomatoes, fennel seeds and tomato purée. Season with salt and pepper and cook the sauce for 10 minutes, until thickened and darker in colour.

4. Meanwhile, cook the spaghetti in a big pan of boiling salted water following the instructions on the pack – it usually takes about 11 minutes.

5. Drain the spaghetti and return it to the hot pan with the spinach and the sausage and tomato sauce. Stir well and allow the heat to wilt the spinach. Serve topped with the Parmesan.

SERVES 4

1 tbsp olive oil
400g sausages
1 onion, peeled and chopped
2 garlic cloves, peeled and crushed
2 x 400g tins chopped tomatoes
1 tsp fennel seeds
2 tbsp tomato purée
300g dried spaghetti
150g baby spinach leaves
sea salt and freshly ground
    black pepper
75g Parmesan cheese, finely grated,
    to serve

Removing the sausages from the outer skins is a bit of a mucky job but it's so worth it as they almost melt into the sauce. You can run a sharp knife along the length of the sausage to remove the skin, if that's easier.

THRIFTY TIP

Substitute Grana Pandano cheese for the Parmesan, if you like. It's still delicious and is usually much cheaper to buy.

15-MINUTE PAPRIKA CHICKEN PASTA

Sweet smoked paprika is one of my favourite spices to have in the cupboard (and not just for the pretty red tin that if often comes in). It's an easy way to add a smoky hit of flavour to so many dishes in next to no time.

1. Cook the pasta in a big pan of boiling salted water following the instructions on the pack – it usually takes about 11 minutes.

2. Meanwhile, heat the oil in a large, deep frying pan over a medium heat. Add the chicken, season with salt and pepper and fry for about 5 minutes, stirring occasionally to make sure the chicken doesn't stick to the bottom of the pan.

3. Add the garlic, peppers, courgettes and paprika to the pan and cook for a further 5 minutes, stirring occasionally, until softened.

4. Turn off the heat under the chicken pan and stir in the cream cheese, lemon juice, tomato purée and a ladleful of the pasta cooking water. Stir the sauce until smooth and heated through, adding more pasta water, if needed

5. Drain the pasta and add it to the sauce. Toss well until combined and serve straight away.

SERVES 4

250g dried pasta
1 tbsp olive oil
600g skinless, boneless chicken breasts, cut into small chunks
2 garlic cloves, peeled and crushed
2 red peppers, deseeded and cut into chunks
2 courgettes, cut into chunks
2 tsp sweet smoked paprika
250g cream cheese
½ lemon, juiced
3 tbsp tomato purée
sea salt and freshly ground black pepper

Make sure you use sweet smoked paprika, rather than the hot version, which can be very spicy.

FAMILY FAVOURITES & FAKEAWAYS

If using meatfree toppings

V ←

CHEAT'S TORTILLA PIZZAS

Since the days of home-schooling, I would guess I've made about a million of these shortcut pizzas. My love for them is enduring for many reasons – they are lighter and quicker than any other pizza, everyone loves them and eats without complaint. My top tip as a tortilla pizza pro (what a title) is to heat the baking sheets in the oven first, which helps to give them a crispy base.

1. Preheat the oven to 200°C fan/220°C/Gas Mark 7. Put 2 large baking sheets in the oven to heat up.

2. Mix the passata with the oregano and garlic granules. Season with salt and pepper.

3. Spread the tomato mixture over each tortilla. Sprinkle with your choice of cheese and toppings.

4. Remove the baking sheets from the oven and very careful lift the pizzas onto the hot baking sheets (you may have to cook them in two batches). Bake for 5–10 minutes, until the cheese melts and the edges of the tortilla are crispy. Serve cut into wedges.

SERVES 4

200ml passata
1 tsp dried oregano
1 tsp garlic granules
4 large soft tortillas
150g grated mozzarella or
    Cheddar cheese
choose your favourite toppings
    (we like slices of pepperoni,
    peppers, mushrooms,
    onions, olives)
sea salt and freshly ground
    black pepper

I find wholemeal tortillas work brilliantly here as they are a little sturdier than those made with white flour.

SERVE WITH
Cheeky Chopped Salad on page 106.

CHEEKY
CHOPPED
SALAD
p. 106

PEANUT PORK NOODLES

The wonder of using peanut butter to make an instant sauce for noodles never fails to please me. It clings onto the noodles for dear life, coating everything in its silky gloss. If you want to reheat leftovers later in the microwave, add an ice cube or two. It will help to rehydrate the noodles and sauce.

250g dried medium egg noodles
2 tbsp sunflower oil
400g boneless pork loins, fat removed and cut into thin strips
1 onion, peeled and thinly sliced
2 green peppers, deseeded and thinly sliced
150g baby sweetcorn, cut in half lengthways
50g roasted peanuts, finely chopped
4 spring onions, sliced into 1cm pieces

For the Peanut Sauce:
150g smooth peanut butter
6 tbsp soy sauce
2 limes, juiced
2 tbsp runny honey
100ml just-boiled water

1. Put the noodles into a large heatproof bowl and cover with just-boiled water from a kettle, stir, then set aside until softened.

2. Meanwhile, make the peanut sauce. Mix the peanut butter with the soy sauce, lime juice and honey in a jug or bowl. As you mix the sauce it will look lumpy and split but keep going and it will come together. Add the boiling water and mix until smooth and a pourable consistency – you may need to add more water. Set aside.

3. Heat the oil in a large, deep frying pan over a high heat. Add the pork strips and cook for 2–3 minutes, stirring often, until starting to colour.

4. Add the vegetables to the pan and cook, stirring, for a further 5 minutes, until cooked through.

5. Check the noodles are soft and cooked through, then drain.

6. Put the drained noodles back into the bowl, add the cooked pork and vegetables and the peanut sauce and turn everything until combined. Serve sprinkled with the roasted peanuts and spring onions.

COCONUT CURRIED SALMON

This tangy, creamy, lightly spiced sauce is the perfect partner for rich salmon. A squeeze of lime at the end and the dish really comes together, ready to be served on top of a bowl of rice.

1. Add the oil, garlic, ginger and curry paste to a large, deep frying pan (with a lid). Cook over a medium heat, stirring and letting it bubble, for about 3 minutes until everything is sizzling and fragrant (this feels a little awkward as there's not much in the pan, but keep going).

2. Add the coconut milk, brown sugar and soy sauce and, using a small balloon whisk, mix until the paste is totally combined.

3. Add the salmon fillets, face down (so skin-side up if your fillets have skin on) to the sauce. Reduce the heat if you need to so the sauce is just bubbling gently and cover with the lid.

4. After 8 minutes, carefully flip the salmon over in the sauce, give each one a sprinkle of pepper and place the green beans around the fillets. Cook for a further 3 minutes, then add the peas around the salmon. Cook for 3 more minutes, until the vegetables are tender and the salmon is cooked through (check by breaking one fillet in the centre).

5. While the salmon is cooking, cook the rice following the instructions on the pack.

6. Squeeze the lime over the salmon and sauce at the end of cooking.

7. Fluff up the rice and spoon into bowls or plates. Top with the vegetables, salmon and spoon the sauce all over.

SERVES 4

1 tsp sunflower oil
3 garlic cloves, peeled and crushed
3 tsp fresh ginger
3 tbsp Thai red curry paste
1 x 400g tin coconut milk
2 tsp soft dark brown sugar
2 tbsp soy sauce
4 salmon fillets (about 500g in total)
200g green beans, trimmed and halved
200g frozen peas
2 x 250g microwave rice pouches (or 300g dry Basmati rice if you have time)
2 limes, halved
sea salt and freshly ground black pepper

Choose salmon fillets with or without skin, whichever you prefer.

THRIFTY TIP

Frozen salmon is often cheaper than fresh, just defrost according to the pack instructions. Of course, you can also cook the rice from scratch, if you prefer – choose long-grain rice.

POT PIE IN A PINCH

Given that food is my language of love, pie is my greatest declaration. The crisp, golden pastry with chunks of tender chicken hidden in a velvety white sauce – it's true comfort food. Thanks to the little trick of cooking the pastry lid separately, I can make my love known, even on a weeknight, in under 30 minutes.

1. Preheat the oven to 200°C fan/220°C/Gas Mark 7.

2. Heat the oil a large, deep frying pan over a medium heat. Add the chicken and cook for 5 minutes, turning occasionally, until browned all over.

3. Add the onion, celery, carrots and thyme to the pan. Season with salt and pepper and cook for 10 minutes, stirring occasionally.

4. Meanwhile, unroll the sheet of puff pastry and cut out whatever shapes you fancy (or cook it in one large sheet, although this will take a little longer). Place on a baking sheet lined with baking paper (you can use the sheet of paper that the pastry comes on) and brush the pastry with the beaten egg. Bake for 10–15 minutes, until golden and crisp.

5. To finish cooking the pie filling, when the chicken and vegetables are cooked stir in the flour and mix until everything is coated. Add the stock, milk and peas and cook for 10 minutes, stirring until the sauce has thickened and everything is heated through.

6. Arrange the cooked pastry shapes on top of the creamy chicken and vegetables, then serve.

SERVES 4

1 tbsp olive oil
650g skinless, boneless chicken breasts, cut into chunks
1 onion, peeled and chopped
3 celery sticks, chopped
3 carrots, peeled and chopped into 1cm pieces
1 tsp dried thyme
320g ready-rolled puff pastry, leave to come to room temperature for 15 minutes
1 egg, lightly beaten
75g plain flour
300ml chicken stock (made with a cube is fine)
300ml whole milk
150g frozen peas
sea salt and freshly ground black pepper

This is a brilliant recipe to make a double portion of and freeze half. Just cook the pie 'filling' and when cool, freeze for up to 3 months. Defrost and reheat until hot through. Cook the pastry and add to the top. (Don't freeze the cooked pastry, but uncooked pastry is a great freezer standby.)

FAMILY FAVOURITES & FAKEAWAYS

CRUNCHY CUTLETS

This is a vague nod to the pork schnitzel – the fried breaded pork cutlet. I love its crispy coating but couldn't face standing over a pan of bubbling oil to make a quick dinner. Here, I use a smear of mustard to secure the lemon breadcrumbs (if you're not a mustard fan, have faith, you can hardly taste it), then the pork loin is baked until golden and crisp.

1. Preheat the oven to 200°C fan/220°C/Gas Mark 7.

2. If the pork fillets have a strip of fat, snip it off with scissors or a sharp knife. Put a pork fillet between 2 sheets of baking paper and bash with the end of a rolling pin or the bottom of a saucepan, until flattened to about 1cm thick. Repeat with all 4 fillets.

3. Put the pork fillets onto a lined baking tray (you can recycle the baking paper you used to flatten them).

4. In a small bowl, mix the breadcrumbs with the lemon zest and olive oil. Season with salt and pepper.

5. Brush the top of each fillet with mustard, then scatter over the breadcrumb mixture, pressing it down so it sticks to both sides of the pork. Bake for 20 minutes, or until cooked through and crunchy on top.

6. Serve the pork with lemon wedges for squeezing over.

SERVES 4

4 pork loin fillets (about **600g** in total), see Tip below
75g dried breadcrumbs, such as panko
1 lemon, zested and cut into wedges
2 tbsp olive oil
2 tsp Dijon mustard
sea salt and freshly ground black pepper

Packs of pork loins seem to vary greatly in thickness and weight – if the ones you buy are very thin, you may need two per person. If this is the case, you'll need extra breadcrumbs.

THRIFTY TIP

To make your own breadcrumbs, freeze any stale bread you have, then grate it. Alternatively, blitz the stale bread in a food processor to coarse crumbs.

SERVE WITH
Warm Waldorf Potatoes on page 106.

FAMILY FAVOURITES & FAKEAWAYS

WARM WALDORF POTATOES
p. 106

SIDES

WARM WALDORF POTATOES

This is a twist on the classic Waldorf salad, but with potatoes added – its fresh crunchy texture works very well with the Crunchy Cutlets (see p.104).

500g new potatoes, scrubbed and halved if large
3 celery sticks, cut into 1cm chunks
2 apples, cored and cut into 1cm chunks
(no need to peel)
1 small or ½ large red onion,
peeled and finely chopped
50g walnuts, roughly chopped

For the Dressing:
50g mayonnaise
75g Greek yoghurt
1 tbsp cider vinegar
sea salt and freshly ground black pepper

Cook the potatoes in boiling salted water for 15 minutes, or until tender. Drain the potatoes and tip them into a serving bowl.

Meanwhile, mix all the ingredients for the dressing together until smooth.

Add the celery, apples, onion and walnuts to the potatoes in the bowl. Pour the dressing over and mix well until everything is combined.

CHEEKY CHOPPED SALAD

The ingredients in this salad are very simple. It's all about the chopping (there's something about the pieces being so small that you get a taste of everything in each bite) and it's more like a salsa than a salad, and surprisingly moreish. I promise, it's worth a little extra chopping time here.

4 large tomatoes (about **240g** in total)
1 medium or ½ large cucumber
1 small red onion

For the Dressing:
1 garlic clove, peeled and crushed
1 tsp Dijon mustard
3 tbsp olive oil, preferably extra-virgin
3 tbsp lemon juice (from 1 or 2 lemons)
½ tsp sea salt

Chop the salad vegetables into 1cm cubes, or even smaller, if preferred. Place in a serving bowl.

Mix all the dressing ingredients together, whisking well until combined. Pour the dressing over the salad just before serving.

MINTY SMASHED AVOCADOS

You'll need to taste this as you go – check for salt, chilli and lime, then adjust to suit your own tastes. The flavour can vary depending on the size and juiciness of the limes and the heat of the chilli sauce.

2 ripe avocados, halved and stoned removed
2 limes, juiced and zested
½ tsp chilli sauce
10g mint, leaves finely chopped
sea salt and freshly ground black pepper

Using a spoon, scoop the avocado flesh into a mixing bowl. Add the lime juice and zest, the chilli sauce and mint. Season with plenty of salt and pepper.

Mash the avocado until combined with the rest of the ingredients – you could use a blender if you prefer a smoother texture or if your avocados aren't quite as ripe as you'd like.

QUICK COLCANNON

I love this shortcut of boiling the potatoes and cabbage together. It feels a bit unnatural to mash everything together, but it's worth getting past that awkwardness to save washing up a second pan.

1kg white potatoes, such as Maris Piper or King Edward, peeled and cut into 3cm chunks
300g Savoy cabbage, outer leaves removed and thinly shredded
30g butter (salted, preferably)
1 tsp wholegrain mustard
sea salt and freshly ground black pepper

Cook the potatoes in a large pan of boiling salted water for 5 minutes.

Add the cabbage and cook for a further 5 minutes, or until the potatoes are cooked through, but not mushy or falling apart.

Drain the potatoes and cabbage well (give them a good shake in the colander so they aren't watery) and return to the pan.

Mash the potatoes and cabbage with the butter, mustard and plenty of salt and pepper.

STICKY GINGER PORK

This sticky, savoury sauce cooks instantly when you pour it into the pan, coating the meat and vegetables. Ready in 15 minutes, hardly any preparation and limited washing up, this quick complete meal is difficult to resist.

SERVES 4

1. To make the sauce, put the cornflour in small bowl and gradually add the soy sauce, stirring to make a paste (adding the liquid a little at a time stops the cornflour turning lumpy). Add the remaining sauce ingredients and stir well. Set aside.

2. In a large, deep frying pan, heat the oil over a high heat and add the pork mince. Fry for 5 minutes, breaking up the mince with a spatula, until the pork starts to colour.

3. Cook the rice according to the packet instructions.

4. To the pork add the ginger purée, garlic, 5-spice and sugar snap peas and fry, stirring, for a further 5 minutes.

5. Turn the heat to low, add the sauce to the pan and cook for 2–5 minutes, stirring, until it thickens and coats the pork. Serve the pork and sauce spooned over rice.

1 tsp sunflower oil
500g pork mince
3 tsp ginger purée
2 garlic cloves, peeled and crushed
1 tsp Chinese 5-spice
200g sugar snap peas
2 x 250g microwave rice pouches (or **300g** dry Basmati rice if you have time)

For the Sauce:
2 tbsp cornflour
3 tbsp soy sauce
3 tbsp runny honey
3 tbsp oyster sauce
1 tbsp white wine vinegar
150ml water

SHEET-PAN STEAK FAJITAS

Everyone loves a fajita, but did you know that you can cook them in the oven, no sweating over the hob? I like to add a tin of black beans to make the portion of steak stretch further and add extra nutrients.

1. Preheat the oven to 200°C fan/220°C/Gas Mark 7.

2. Put the steak, onion, peppers and black beans on a baking tray and drizzle the oil over.

3. Mix all the ingredients together for the fajita seasoning (if you are making your own). Sprinkle the seasoning over the steak, beans and vegetables and toss with your hands until everything is combined and coated in the seasoned oil. Cook for 10–12 minutes in the oven, or until the steak is cooked to your liking.

4. Meanwhile warm the tortillas – I like to hold them very carefully with tongs over a gas hob until blackened in places, otherwise wrap them in foil and warm in the oven.

5. Serve the tortillas, steak, beans and vegetables at the table and let everyone pile in.

450g sirloin steak, fat removed and cut into long 1cm strips
1 onion, peeled and thinly sliced
3 peppers (your colour of choice), deseeded and cut into thin strips
1 x 400g tin black beans, drained and rinsed
3 tbsp olive oil

For the Fajita Seasoning:
(or use **2 tbsp** of ready-made fajita seasoning):
1 tsp ground cumin
2 tsp paprika
¼ tsp cayenne pepper
½ tsp garlic granules
1 tsp sea salt
1 tsp freshly ground black pepper

To Serve:
8 small tortilla wraps
yoghurt or soured cream
grated Cheddar cheese

SERVE WITH
Minty Smashed Avocados page 107.

MINTY SMASHED
AVOCADOS
p. 107

HAWAIIAN-STYLE PORK

I must confess, I am in the 'not-for-me' camp when it comes to fruit on a pizza, but fruit in a heavenly sticky, savoury sauce and in under 20 minutes – this I am very much a fan of. Make sure the vegetables are still crunchy when you've cooked them if you can.

1. Heat the oil in a large, deep frying pan over a medium heat. Add the pork and paprika. Season with plenty of salt and pepper and cook for 10 minutes, stirring occasionally, until the pork is browned all over.

2. Meanwhile, make the sauce. Put the cornflour into a measuring jug and add a spoonful or two of juice from the can of pineapple, then mix to a paste. (Set aside the pineapple chunks to add with the vegetables.) Mix the remaining pineapple juice, sugar, garlic and ground ginger into the jug. The amount of sauce should measure about 150ml (depending on the amount of juice in the canned pineapple), then top it up to 300ml in total with water.

3. Cook the rice following the instructions on the pack.

4. Add the baby sweetcorn, green pepper and the saved pineapple chunks to the pan with the pork and cook for a further 2–3 minutes.

5. Turn the heat to high, pour the sauce into the pan and cook for 5 minutes, stirring occasionally, until the sauce has thickened, and the pork is cooked through.

6. Serve the pork over the cooked rice.

1 tbsp sunflower oil
500g pork tenderloin, trimmed of fat and cut into 3cm chunks
2 tsp sweet smoked paprika
200g baby sweetcorn, halved
1 green pepper, deseeded and cut into thin strips
sea salt and freshly ground black pepper
2 x 250g microwave rice pouches (or **300g** dry Basmati rice if you have time), to serve

For the Sauce:
2½ tsp cornflour
1 x 260g tin pineapple chunks in juice, drained but save the juice
1 tsp light brown soft sugar
2 garlic cloves, peeled and crushed
1 tsp ground ginger
approx. **150ml** water

GARLIC FETA LOADED SALMON

This is one of those meals where the result feels like more than just a sum of its parts – something about the salty, crumbly feta with the oily fish and juicy roasted courgettes. It comes together without too much effort at all and manages to look very pretty on the plate too.

SERVES 4

3 tsp olive oil
200g feta cheese, crumbled
2 tsp garlic granules
1 tsp dried oregano
1 lemon, zested and halved
4 salmon fillets (about **500g** in total)
3 large courgettes, cut into 3cm chunks
240g couscous
360ml hot vegetable stock (made with a cube is fine)
3 tbsp green pesto
sea salt and freshly ground black pepper

1. Preheat the oven to 180°C fan/200°C/Gas Mark 6.

2. In a small bowl, mix 2 teaspoons of the oil with the feta, garlic granules, oregano and the zest of the lemon. Season with salt and pepper and mash with a fork until the feta is finely crumbled and everything is combined.

3. Put the salmon on a baking tray, skin side down, and spoon the feta mixture on top of each fillet.

4. Arrange the courgettes around the salmon and drizzle over the remaining oil. Season with salt and pepper and place the lemon halves on the tray too. Bake for 15 minutes, or until the salmon is cooked through and the courgettes are tender.

5. Meanwhile, put the couscous into a large heatproof bowl, pour the stock over and stir in the pesto. Cover with a plate and leave to one side. Leave for about 10 minutes, until the stock is absorbed. Fluff the couscous up with a fork and combine with the courgettes.

6. Spoon the courgette couscous onto serving plates and top with the salmon. Squeeze the roasted lemon over everything before serving.

LAZY LAMB TAGINE

A fragrant tagine is one of my favourite dishes – the tender meat and rich, fragrant sauce instantly transport me to an exotic souk a million miles from day-to-day life. A traditional Moroccan tagine should be cooked very slowly with chunks of meat and a delicate blend of spices. Here, I've added a couple of shortcuts to make this meal achievable, even on a weeknight; minced lamb, which cooks much quicker than chunks, and the brilliant spice blend, ras el hanout. The spice blend is available in most large supermarkets and is worth seeking out.

1. In a large dry saucepan over a medium heat, fry off the lamb for 5 minutes (you shouldn't need any oil as it tends to have plenty of its own fat), stirring with a wooden spoon to break up the mince, until it starts to brown.

2. Add the onion, garlic, butternut squash and ras el hanout, stir well, and cook for a further 5 minutes.

3. Add the chopped tomatoes, then half-fill the can with water and add to the pan with the tomato purée. Season with salt and pepper and give everything a good stir. Cover with the lid and cook over a medium heat for 20 minutes, stirring occasionally.

4. Meanwhile, put the couscous in a large heatproof bowl, pour over the hot stock and cover with a plate. Leave to sit for 10 minutes, until the stock is absorbed.

5. Fluff up the couscous with a fork and spoon onto serving plates. Serve the tagine spooned on top, sprinkled with flaked almonds.

SERVES 4

500g lamb mince
1 onion, peeled and chopped
2 garlic cloves, peeled and crushed
350g butternut squash, peeled and cut into 2cm cubes
4 tsp ras el hanout spice mix
1 x 400g tin chopped tomatoes
2 tbsp tomato purée
sea salt and freshly ground black pepper

To Serve:
240g couscous
360ml hot vegetable stock (made with a cube is fine)
25g flaked almonds

This dish freezes brilliantly if you fancy making a double batch.

Ras el hanout spice mix seems to vary in strength. You may want to start with 4 teaspoons and add more as it cooks if you feel it's not flavourful enough.

To save time, use pre-chopped or frozen butternut squash.

NO-STIR CHORIZO RISOTTO

There are few meals quite as comforting as a bowl of creamy risotto, but who can face stirring a pan continuously when time is short? I often use this method of popping the pan of rice into the oven to cook – the finished risotto is slightly different to one cooked on the hob but it's so much easier and makes a delicious complete meal.

1. Preheat the oven to 200°C fan/220°C/Gas Mark 7.

2. Heat a large, heavy-based, ovenproof saucepan (with a lid) over a high heat. Add the chorizo and cook for 2–3 minutes, until the oils start to run out.

3. Turn the heat down to medium and add the onion and garlic and cook for another 2–3 minutes, until the onion starts to soften.

4. Next, add the rice and paprika and stir everything together until the rice is well coated. Cook for a couple of minutes, stirring, until the rice starts to look shiny.

5. Add the stock and chopped tomatoes. Season with plenty of salt and pepper and give everything a good stir. Cover with the lid and pop the pan in the oven for 20 minutes.

6. Add the frozen peas, give everything a good stir, and pop back in the oven for a further 5 minutes, until the rice is cooked and tender.

7. Remove the pan from the oven, stir in the butter and check for seasoning. You can then either stir the Parmesan through the risotto or sprinkle it on top before serving.

SERVES 4

225g chorizo (the type in a ring), cut into 2cm chunks
1 large onion, peeled and chopped
2 garlic cloves, peeled and crushed
300g arborio risotto rice
2 tsp sweet smoked paprika
1 litre hot vegetable stock (from a cube is fine)
1 x 400g tin chopped tomatoes
200g frozen peas
sea salt and freshly ground black pepper

To Serve:
50g butter
75g Parmesan cheese, finely grated

SAUSAGE & MASH WITH A SECRET

The 'secret' is that hidden on this plate are not one, but two sneaky portions of veg per person. You don't have to blend the onion gravy, but for many years my children could spot even the smallest piece of onion and be mortally offended by it. I'm a big fan of using pre-chopped onions for speed – they also seem to cook down more quickly into the gravy – but feel free to chop your own if you prefer.

1. **Make a start on the mash. Cook the parsnips in a large pan of boiling salted water for 5 minutes. Add the potatoes and cook for a further 15–18 minutes, until very soft but not falling apart.**

2. **Meanwhile, heat the oil in a large, deep frying pan over a medium heat. Add the sausages and cook for 10 minutes, turning occasionally, until they start to colour all over. (Pop the lid on if your pan has one and shuffle them around occasionally.)**

3. **Remove the lid, add the onions and cook for a further 10 minutes, stirring regularly, until golden (you may need to turn the heat down to low if the onions start to catch on the bottom of the pan).**

4. **Drain the potatoes and parsnips when cooked and return to the pan. Add the butter and plenty of salt and pepper and mash until smooth. Set aside.**

5. **When the sausages are cooked, remove them from the pan and set aside, leaving the onions. Stir the flour into the pan to coat the onions and cook for 2–3 minutes.**

6. **Turn the heat up to medium-high, add the beef stock and Worcestershire sauce and let the gravy bubble and thicken for 3–5 minutes, stirring occasionally. You can blend the gravy at this point with a hand-held blender until smooth.**

7. **Spoon the mash onto serving plates, top with the sausages and pour the gravy over.**

SERVES 4

2 tsp sunflower oil
8 pork sausages
2 onions, peeled and chopped (about **400g**, if you are using pre chopped)
75g plain flour
750ml hot beef stock (made with a cube is fine)
3 tbsp Worcestershire sauce

For the Mash:
500g parsnips, peeled and cut into 3cm cubes
1kg white potatoes, peeled and cut into 3cm cubes
50g butter (preferably salted)
sea salt and freshly ground black pepper

Freeze any leftover gravy for use another time.

FRIDAY NIGHT FRIED RICE

When the need for a 'hurray-it's-the-weekend' takeaway arrives, my option is quicker than waiting for a delivery – not to mention lighter and cheaper. It pays to keep a supply of the ingredients in the freezer, and you'll always have a takeaway-style dinner at your fingertips in less than 15 minutes.

1. Heat the oil in a large, deep, heavy-based frying pan over a high heat. Add the prawns, garlic, mixed vegetables, 5-spice and fry for 5 minutes, stirring.

2. Tip in the rice (no need to microwave it first), breaking it up as you go if it is in lumps. Add the oyster sauce and soy sauce and cook for a further 5 minutes. Keep stirring to break up the rice.

3. Make a couple of wells in the mixture and divide the beaten eggs between each one. Leave the eggs to cook for 1 minute, then stir the eggs into the rice mixture until combined and cooked – they take about 5 minutes.

4. Sprinkle with the chopped spring onions before serving.

SERVES 4

2 tsp sunflower oil
400g frozen large raw peeled prawns
2 garlic cloves, peeled and crushed
450g mixed frozen vegetables
1 tbsp Chinese 5-spice
2 x 250g microwave rice pouches
2 tbsp oyster sauce
2 tbsp dark soy sauce
4 eggs, lightly beaten
3 spring onions, chopped

THRIFTY TIP

Swap the prawns for leftover slices of roast meat, chicken or ham.

HOTPOT IN A HURRY

No, it's not glamorous but this is the ultimate in easy comfort food – warming and cosy, crispy potatoes on top, hiding a gravy-drenched filling below. If you do have extra time, let the meat filling cook a little longer, it will thank you for it. This hotpot has enough veg to make a complete meal, but growing up we always ate baked beans and HP sauce on the side of dishes like this. I'm still a fan of those if you fancy the full experience.

1. Heat 2 teaspoons of the oil in a large, deep frying pan over a high heat (it needs to be suitable to go under the grill). Add the mince and cook, stirring to break up the mince with a wooden spoon, for 5 minutes, until starting to brown.

2. While the beef is browning, cook the potato slices in a large pan of boiling salted water for 8–10 minutes, or until soft. Drain and set aside.

3. To the mince, add the onion, garlic, leeks, carrots and thyme and cook for a further 5 minutes, stirring occasionally.

4. Add the flour to the mince mixture and stir until everything is well coated. Next, add the stock, tomato purée and Worcestershire sauce. Season with salt and pepper. Turn the heat to medium-low, cover with the lid and cook for 15 minutes, stirring occasionally, until the sauce has thickened slightly.

5. Meanwhile, preheat the grill to high.

6. When the mince filling is cooked, layer the potatoes on top and drizzle the remaining oil over. Pop under the grill for 5 minutes, until the potatoes are crisp.

SERVES 4

3 tsp sunflower oil
500g beef mince (about 10% fat)
750g white potatoes, such as Maris Piper or King Edward, peeled and cut into 1cm thick round slices
1 onion, peeled and finely chopped
3 garlic cloves, peeled and chopped
2 leeks, finely chopped
2 carrots, peeled and finely chopped
2 tsp dried thyme
75g plain flour
450ml beef stock
4 tbsp tomato purée
4 tbsp Worcestershire sauce
plenty of sea salt and freshly ground black pepper

You can layer the potatoes on top of the mince in the same deep frying pan if it's suitable for use under the grill (watch out for plastic handles, I've melted one before!). Otherwise, transfer to a grill-proof roasting dish and layer the potatoes on top.

STICKY GAMMON STEAKS

I'm not sure why gammon steaks seem to have fallen out of favour of late, who wouldn't want a giant slab of bacon for dinner? Not only do they have a long use-by date in the fridge as they are vacuum packed, but they also cook very quickly under the grill.

1. Preheat the grill to medium.

2. Take the gammon steaks out of the pack and cut off the rinds, if needed. Snip a few cuts into the fat – this stops the steaks curling as they cook.

3. Rub the gammon steaks all over with the oil and the Chinese 5-spice and grill for 4 minutes on one side.

4. Flip the gammon over, dollop a teaspoon of marmalade on top of each one and return the steaks to the grill for a further 4–6 minutes, until cooked through and the marmalade is sticky and golden.

SERVES 4

4 gammon steaks (about **800g** in total), see Thrifty Tip below
2 tsp sunflower oil
2 tsp Chinese 5-spice
4 tsp marmalade

THRIFTY TIP

If you're cooking this for young children, I'd reduce the quantity of gammon as the steaks are quite large – annoyingly they usually come in packs of two. You could freeze one steak for another day or cook it and use the leftovers in another meal.

SERVE WITH
Quick Colcannon on page 107.

QUICK COLCANNON
p. 107

FISH PIE IN A FLASH

Fish pie is a forever family favourite, but if you're not in the mood for peeling lots of potatoes, here is a super shortcut using filo pastry for the top instead. My pack of filo contained 7 sheets and I used half of them, leaving enough in the freezer for a second pie another day.

1. Preheat the oven to 180°C fan/200°C/Gas Mark 6.

2. Warm the milk in a medium-sized saucepan over a low heat.

3. In a mug or small bowl, mix the cornflour with the remaining 2 tablespoons of milk to a smooth paste, then add to the pan. Stir over a low heat until the milk starts to thicken, about 5 minutes.

4. Add the parsley, peas and the fish pie mix. Stir it very gently (so you don't break up the fish) and cook for 5 minutes, or until the fish is just cooked through.

5. Stir in the cooked prawns and pour the mixture carefully into a shallow ovenproof dish.

6. Cut each sheet of filo pastry into 3 or 4 long strips and scrunch them up on top of the fish mixture.

7. Drizzle the oil over the pastry and bake in the oven for 15–20 minutes, until the filo is golden and crisp.

SERVES 4

500ml whole milk,
plus an extra 2 tbsp
30g cornflour
10g fresh flat-leaf parsley,
leaves finely chopped
300g frozen peas
640g fish pie mix
150g cooked prawns
135g filo pastry, about 3–4 sheets
2 tsp sunflower oil
sea salt and freshly ground
black pepper

You can use raw prawns, if you prefer, just add them to the filling when you add the fish pie mix and check they are pink and cooked through before serving.

THRIFTY TIP

Any leftover filo pastry from the pack can be frozen for use another day.

SERVE WITH
Minty Greens, see opposite.

MINTY GREENS

MINTY GREENS

Despite this dish sounding like the name of a soap opera character, it is a surprise winner here. Cooking cabbage in butter brings out its sweetness, and the addition of mint is just enough to add a little zing to proceedings.

50g salted butter
1 Savoy cabbage, outer leaves removed and shredded
2 tsp mint sauce (the vinegary type, not mint jelly)
sea salt and freshly ground black pepper

Melt the butter in a large saucepan over a medium heat. Add the cabbage and stir for 2–3 minutes until it's coated in the butter.

Turn the heat down to low, add 100ml water, cover with the lid and cook for 15–20 minutes, or until the cabbage is tender. Stir in the mint sauce and season with salt and pepper.

FULLY LOADED FISH NAAN

When we are trying to eat quickly, tasty bread is an ideal solution – here naan bread does just the job. Spiced fish and veggies are piled on top of the naan to look something like a sort of pizza, perhaps. Eat with a knife and fork, or better still, roll it up with the fish inside and eat with your hands.

1. Preheat the oven to 200°C fan/220°C/Gas Mark 7.

2. Put the cod, onion, peppers and tomatoes into a large bowl. Drizzle over the oil, garam masala, cumin and garlic granules and gently turn to coat everything in the spiced oil. (Be careful not to break up the fish; it's easier to do this with clean hands if you can).

3. Spread the fish and vegetables out on a baking tray lined with baking paper. Bake at the top of the oven for about 15 minutes or until the fish is cooked through and the vegetables are softened.

4. Meanwhile, mix all the ingredients for the dressing together.

5. Warm the naan breads according to the instructions on the pack (I usually put them in the oven 5 minutes before the fish is cooked).

6. Serve the naan topped with the fish fillets and vegetables, drizzled with the yoghurt dressing.

SERVES 4

4 cod fillets or other white fish (about **500g** in total)
1 onion, peeled and cut into wedges
3 peppers (your colour of choice), deseeded and cut into thick slices
2 large tomatoes, (about **120g** in total) cut into quarters
2 tbsp sunflower oil
4 tsp garam masala
4 tsp ground cumin
2 tsp garlic granules
4 naan breads, to serve

For the Yoghurt Dressing:
200ml natural yoghurt
3 tsp mint sauce (the vinegary type, not mint jelly)
1 tsp ground cumin
1 cucumber, chopped into 1cm cubes
pinch of sea salt

Keep a supply of naan bread in the freezer – they can be warmed in the oven from frozen when needed.

THRIFTY TIP

Frozen fish fillets are almost always cheaper than fresh. Use frozen fish and adjust the cooking time according to the pack instructions (or defrost first if recommended on the pack).

FAMILY FAVOURITES & FAKEAWAYS

BROCCOLI & BACON BAKE

This dish is unashamedly a result of growing up in the 80s – carbs, bacon and cheese, what's not to love? It's comfort food at its finest and if you manage to have any leftovers, the bake is such a treat to find in the fridge the next day.

1. Preheat the oven to 200°C fan/220°C/Gas Mark 7.

2. Cook the potatoes in a large pan of boiling salted water for 8 minutes. Add the broccoli to the pan and cook for a further 7 minutes, or until the potatoes are tender. Drain and return them to the pan.

3. Meanwhile, heat the oil in a medium-sized, non-stick saucepan over a medium heat. Add the bacon and fry for 5 minutes, stirring occasionally, until starting to colour.

4. Add the onion to the bacon and cook for a further 5 minutes, stirring occasionally, until softened.

5. In a mug, mix the cornflour with 2 tablespoons of the milk to a smooth paste (this stops the sauce going lumpy).

6. To the bacon and onions, add the remaining milk, the cornflour paste, the garlic granules, mustard and half of the cheese. Season with salt and pepper. Turn the heat to low and cook for 10 minutes, stirring often, until thickened to a delicious sauce.

7. Pour the sauce into the pan containing the cooked potatoes and broccoli and stir until combined, then transfer to an ovenproof dish. Scatter over the remaining cheese and bake for about 5–10 minutes, until golden on top and heated through.

750g white potatoes, such as Maris Piper or King Edward, cut into 2cm cubes (no need to peel)
1 head of broccoli (about **225g**), cut into small pieces
1 tsp sunflower oil
200g smoked bacon lardons
1 onion, peeled and chopped
30g cornflour
500ml whole milk
1 tsp garlic granules
1 tsp wholegrain mustard
150g mature Cheddar cheese, coarsely grated
sea salt and freshly ground black pepper

THRIFTY TIP

Frozen broccoli is a good option here instead of fresh, but cook it for slightly less time, about 2–4 minutes.

ONE-POT CAJUN-STYLE CHICKEN & RICE

Complete dinner, all in one pan? Yes please. This quick and tasty rice dish will be a new favourite, not least because of the minimum of washing up involved. It also happens to be tasty, packed with vegetables and low on effort as well as the number of ingredients required. Always a win!

1. Heat the oil in a large, deep frying pan over a medium heat. Add the chicken and cook for 2 minutes, stirring often, until sealed all over and starting to colour.

2. Add the onion, garlic, celery, green peppers and Cajun seasoning and cook for 5 minutes, until the vegetables start to soften.

3. Add the rice to the pan with the tomato purée and stock. Season with salt and pepper and give everything a good stir. Pop the lid on and cook for 15–20 minutes, stirring occasionally, until the rice has soaked up the stock and the chicken is cooked through.

4. Fluff up the rice with a fork and served sprinkled with the spring onions, if using.

1 tbsp olive oil
500g skinless, boneless chicken breasts, cut into small chunks
1 onion, peeled and chopped
3 garlic cloves, peeled and crushed
3 celery sticks, cut into small chunks
2 green peppers, deseeded and cut into small chunks
4 tsp Cajun seasoning
200g long-grain rice, rinsed
4 tbsp tomato purée
800ml chicken stock
6 spring onions, chopped (optional)

The level of Cajun spicing here should be fairly mild and suitable for children (unless you've bought a particularly fiery spice mix!), but if you'd like more heat, add another teaspoon or so.

BRILLIANT BOWLS & HEALTHY TWISTS

SALMON BITE BOWLS

The best 'bowl' recipes should be super simple – their charm is in the colourful presentation and, of course, the small amount of time they take to put together. This bowl is definitely more than the sum of its parts. I find cutting the salmon into cubes is totally worth the extra 5 minutes it takes and means that the fish becomes deliciously crispy and golden all over when fried.

1. Add 1 teaspoon of the oil to a mixing bowl with the paprika and garlic granules. Season with salt and pepper and mix everything together to combine. Add the salmon and gently turn to coat it in the spice mix. Set aside.

2. Make the sweet chilli mayonnaise by mixing all the ingredients together in a small bowl. Set aside.

3. Heat the remaining 1 teaspoon of oil in a large frying pan over a high heat. When it's hot, add the salmon and cook for about 10 minutes until lightly golden all over – don't shuffle it around too much or the chunks will break up.

4. While the salmon is cooking, cook the rice following the instructions on the pack.

5. Using a vegetable peeler, cut the carrots and cucumber into thin ribbons.

6. Pile the rice into 4 serving bowls and top with the carrots, cucumber, avocado and salmon, then give everything a good squeeze of lime. Drizzle over the sweet chilli mayo before serving.

2 tsp sunflower oil
1 tsp paprika
1 tsp garlic granules
500g skinless salmon fillets, bones removed, cut into 3cm cubes
sea salt and freshly ground black pepper

To Serve:
2 x 250g microwave rice pouches (or **300g** dry Basmati rice if you have time)
3 carrots, peeled
½ cucumber
1 avocado, halved, peeled, stone removed and cut into slices
2 limes, halved

For the Sweet Chilli Mayo:
60g mayonnaise
1 tbsp sweet chilli sauce
1 lime, juiced

THRIFTY TIP

Fresh salmon can be expensive, so it's worth looking out for frozen, which is usually cheaper, then cook following the pack instructions.

15-MINUTE FISH TACOS

I have yet to taste a flavour of taco I didn't like, and this recipe is no exception. Fish tacos often use fried battered fish, but here I bake the fish in the oven, making the tacos quicker and lighter. It's simple, such an easy way to encourage children to try fish, and the zingy slaw works so well with it too. You can adjust the fish seasoning to use a little less if your family aren't a big fan of spicy food.

1. Preheat the oven to 180°C fan/200°C/Gas Mark 6.

2. Put the fish fillets on a baking sheet and rub all over with the oil and Cajun seasoning. Bake for 13–15 minutes, or until cooked through.

3. Meanwhile, combine all the ingredients for the slaw and set aside.

4. Warm your tortillas – I like to hold them very carefully with tongs directly over the gas hob for a couple of seconds to char them a little. You can also warm the tortillas in the oven – wrap them in a foil parcel, then place in the oven for 5 minutes with the fish.

5. When the fish is cooked, break the fillets into big chunks.

6. Serve the tacos topped with the slaw, avocado and the fish chunks – letting everyone help themselves.

SERVES 4

500g white fish fillets, without skin
2 tsp sunflower oil
3 tsp Cajun seasoning

For the Slaw:
½ red cabbage, finely shredded
1 red onion, finely shredded
2 tbsp jalapeños from a jar, roughly chopped (optional)
2 tsp runny honey
150g natural yoghurt
2 limes, juiced and zested

To Serve:
8 small tortilla wraps
1 avocado, halved, peeled, stone removed and sliced

THRIFTY TIP

Frozen fish fillets are almost always cheaper than fresh. You will need to adjust the cooking time according to the pack instructions (or defrost first if recommended on the pack).

BRILLIANT BOWLS & HEALTHY TWISTS

BUILD-YOUR-OWN BURRITO BOWLS

I call this 'build-your-own' as I like to put separate plates of everything on the table and let people help themselves to create their own perfect bowl combo. For fussy eaters, this is a great way to encourage them to try new things without putting too much pressure on them. You can also serve this with tortilla wraps, if you fancy, to make rolled-up burritos.

1. Heat the oil in a large frying pan over a medium-high heat. Add the chicken and Cajun or fajita seasoning. Season with salt and pepper and cook for 10–12 minutes, stirring often, until the chicken pieces are cooked through.

2. Meanwhile, cook the rice following the instructions on the pack and divide between 4 bowls.

3. Top the rice with the sweetcorn, black beans, avocado and salsa.

4. When the chicken is cooked, spoon it on top of each serving and give everything a good squeeze of lime. Serve with the tortilla chips on the side.

2 tbsp sunflower oil
500g skinless, boneless chicken breasts, cut into small chunks
4 tsp Cajun or fajita seasoning
sea salt and freshly ground black pepper

To Serve:
2 x 250g microwave rice pouches (or **300g** dry Basmati rice if you have time)
1 x 325g tin sweetcorn, drained
1 x 400g tin black beans, drained and rinsed
1 avocado, halved, stone removed, peeled and sliced
200g fresh tomato salsa (from the supermarket dips section)
2 limes, halved
100g tortilla chips

If you prefer, heat the sweetcorn and black beans in the microwave or a small pan before adding to your bowls.

BACON & CORN CHOWDER

This soup is the stuff of legend in our family. It's so good that my children still talk about the day that they ate three bowls each: one as a starter, one as a main course, and one for pudding. Could there be any higher recommendation? It's a complete meal in a bowl, and somehow gives the impression that you've carefully crafted it over hours, rather than in 20 minutes. Of course, it's best served with crusty bread for dunking (as most things are).

1. Add the oil and bacon to a large saucepan over a medium heat and fry, stirring occasionally, for 5 minutes, until the bacon starts to colour.

2. Add the onion, garlic and potatoes, give everything a good stir, and let the vegetables cook for a further 5 minutes. Stir in the flour to coat the vegetables.

3. Add the smoked paprika, chicken stock and milk. Season with salt and pepper and cook over a medium-low heat for 10 minutes, stirring occasionally.

4. Add the sweetcorn and cook for a further 5–10 minutes, or until the potatoes are cooked through.

5. Before serving, I like to use a hand-held blender to partially blend the soup in the pan. I leave plenty of big chunks of potato and blend it just enough to thicken the soup. Ladle into bowls and serve with crusty bread.

SERVES 4

1 tbsp sunflower oil
200g smoked bacon lardons
1 onion, peeled and chopped
3 garlic cloves, peeled and crushed
750g white potatoes, like Maris Piper or King Edward, cut into 2cm chunks (no need to peel)
75g plain flour
1 tsp sweet smoked paprika
750ml hot chicken stock
250ml whole milk
2 x 325g tins sweetcorn, drained and rinsed (or use frozen)
sea salt and freshly ground black pepper

This soup freezes well, but when reheated you may need to thin it a little with water or milk.

THRIFTY TIP

You can use regular smoked bacon instead of lardons – just snip into pieces with scissors.

GREEK CHICKEN BOWLS

I know this list of ingredients looks longer than my usual, but please keep the faith. It's mainly just an assembly job so the bowls look and taste far more fancy than the effort needed to make them; while your meatballs are baking, pile everything else together. Leftovers of this are a joy to discover in the fridge the next day.

SERVES 4

For the Meatballs:
500g chicken mince
1 egg
40g dried breadcrumbs,
    such as panko
1 red onion, finely chopped
2 tsp dried oregano
100g feta cheese, crumbled
sea salt and freshly ground
    black pepper

For the Yoghurt Dip:
200g Greek yoghurt
2 tsp mint sauce (the vinegary type,
    not mint jelly)
½ cucumber, grated (squeeze
    the water out with your hands
    after grating)
pinch of sea salt

To Serve:
2 x 250g microwave rice pouches
    (or **300g** dry Basmati rice if
    you have time)
200g cherry tomatoes, halved
½ cucumber, chopped into
    small chunks
100g pitted black olives (optional)
100g feta cheese, crumbled
4 tsp extra-virgin olive oil

1. Preheat the oven to 180°C fan/200°C/Gas Mark 6.

2. Mix all the meatball ingredients together in a bowl. Using clean hands, shape the mixture into 20 small meatballs, about the size of a walnut, and place on a baking tray lined with baking paper. Bake the meatballs for 15–20 minutes, or until cooked through.

3. Meanwhile, make the yoghurt dip by mixing all the ingredients in a bowl.

4. Cook the rice according to the instructions on the pack and divide between 4 bowls.

5. Top the rice with the cherry tomatoes, cucumber, olives, if using, feta cheese and a dollop of the yoghurt dip.

6. When the meatballs are cooked, add five to each bowl and serve with an extra drizzle of olive oil.

NAKED BURRITO RICE

A burrito, without the... burrito! This rice dish is ready in 15 minutes – and you only need one pan. If you prefer your burrito 'fully clothed', feel free to stuff the filling inside warm tortilla wraps.

1. Heat the oil in a large, deep frying pan over a medium heat. Add the mince and cook for 10 minutes, stirring to break it up with a wooden spoon, until browned all over.

2. Add the garlic, paprika and cumin and cook, stirring occasionally, for a further 5 minutes.

3. Meanwhile, cook the rice following the instructions on the pack.

4. Add the hot rice, sweetcorn, black beans and tomato purée to the mince mixture. Pour in 100ml water and season with salt and pepper, then give everything a good stir and cook for 5 minutes, until heated through.

5. Before serving, stir through the salsa and scatter over the spring onions, if using. Serve in bowls with wedges of lime for squeezing over.

SERVES 4

2 tsp sunflower oil
500g lean beef mince
3 garlic cloves, peeled and crushed
3 tsp paprika
2 tsp ground cumin
2 x 250g microwave rice pouches (or **300g** dry Basmati rice if you have time)
1 x 325g tin sweetcorn, drained
1 x 400g tin black beans, drained
2 tbsp tomato purée
200g fresh tomato salsa (from the supermarket dips aisle)
2 spring onions, chopped (optional)
sea salt and freshly ground black pepper
2 limes, cut into wedges, to finish

You can add the pouches of rice straight to the pan without heating them first in the microwave, if you prefer. Make sure you break up the rice as it does have a tendency to stick together and heat it through thoroughly.

BRILLIANT BOWLS & HEALTHY TWISTS

MOROCCAN-STYLE CHICKEN WITH COUSCOUS

These mild, sweet spices used to coat the chicken and peppers are one of my favourite combinations. If you have a meat thermometer, use it to check that the chicken is cooked through as cooking times can vary greatly, depending on the size and shape of the pieces – not being overcooked makes such a difference to the result.

1. Preheat the oven to 180°C fan/200°C/Gas Mark 6.

2. Mix all the ingredients for the spice paste in a small bowl.

3. Put the chicken and peppers onto a baking tray and cover in the spice paste – it's easiest to do this using clean hands to make sure everything is well coated. Bake for 20–25 minutes, until the chicken is cooked through and golden, and the peppers have softened.

4. Meanwhile, put the couscous into a large heatproof bowl and pour over the hot stock. Add the apricots and season with salt and pepper. Mix until combined, cover with a plate, and leave for about 10 minutes to allow the couscous to absorb the stock.

5. When the couscous is ready, fluff it up with a fork, then mix in the roasted peppers. Spoon into 4 bowls.

6. Slice the chicken breasts and arrange them on top of the couscous and serve.

SERVES 4

4 skinless, boneless chicken breasts (about **600g** in total)
3 peppers (colour of choice), deseeded and cut into chunks
240g couscous
360ml hot vegetable stock (made with a cube is fine)
75g dried apricots, cut into very small pieces
sea salt and freshly ground black pepper

For the Spice Paste:
3 tsp ground cumin
1 tsp ground cinnamon
3 tsp paprika
1 tsp ground turmeric
4 tbsp sunflower oil

If you have a spare 10 minutes, let the chicken rest, covered, before cutting it up – this helps to retain the juices.

Serve with a dollop of yoghurt if you fancy.

HONEY & LIME TURKEY NOODLE BOWL

Turkey isn't just for Christmas – it's cooked here in a zesty fresh sauce with heaps of green vegetables for texture and flavour. If chicken has been a staple of your regular meal plans, turkey is a simple way to mix things up a little.

SERVES 4

1. Put the egg noodles in a large heatproof bowl and pour over boiling water to cover. Stir to separate the noodles and set aside, covered with a plate, to let them soften.

2. Meanwhile, make the sauce. Mix the cornflour with the hoisin sauce in a small jug or bowl until smooth. Add the remaining sauce ingredients and set aside.

3. Heat the oil in a large, deep frying pan over a high heat. Add the turkey, sprinkle over the 5-spice to coat and fry for 3–5 minutes, until lightly golden.

4. Add the sugar snap peas and cabbage and fry for a further 3–5 minutes, until everything is cooked through.

5. Pour the sauce over the turkey and vegetables and allow to bubble for 5 minutes, until thickened, then turn off the heat.

6. Check that the noodles are cooked, then drain and add to the pan. Toss until everything is combined. Serve in bowls with extra soy sauce, if you like.

250g dried medium egg noodles
1 tbsp sunflower oil
400g turkey steaks, cut into thin strips
2 tsp Chinese 5-spice
150g sugar snap peas
250g Savoy cabbage, finely shredded
soy sauce, to serve (optional)

For the Sauce:
1 tbsp cornflour
75g hoisin sauce
2 limes, juiced and zested
4 tbsp runny honey
3 garlic cloves, crushed
100ml water

CRISPY PESTO COD

This combination of pesto, smoky prosciutto and flaky white fish is something special. This dish also accidentally looks very impressive. It makes a satisfyingly fancy looking dish for serving to friends or dishing up on a date night.

SERVES 4

6 tsp pesto
4 cod fillets (about **500g** in total)
90g prosciutto (about 6 thin slices)
200g long-stem broccoli
2 tsp olive oil
2 lemons, juiced and zested
sea salt and freshly ground
    black pepper

1. Preheat the oven to 180°C fan/200°C/Gas Mark 6.

2. Spoon 1 teaspoon of the pesto over the top of each cod fillet and spread it out evenly to cover.

3. Wrap each cod fillet in 1½ slices of prosciutto. Place the fish on one side of a large baking tray lined with baking paper.

4. Place the broccoli on the other side of the tray. Mix the remaining 2 teaspoons of pesto with the olive oil and lemon zest in a small bowl. Season with salt and pepper and drizzle all over the broccoli.

5. Bake for 10–15 minutes, until the prosciutto is crisp, and the fish is cooked through. Give everything a good squeeze of lemon juice and serve.

The cooking time for fish fillets can vary a lot depending on their thickness, which makes timing difficult to gauge. Thinner fillets are likely to take about 10 minutes, while thicker ones may need about 15 minutes – just check they are cooked through before serving.

SERVE WITH
Garlic & Herb Mash on page 158.

GARLIC & HERB MASH
p. 158

STICKY TURKEY TACOS

Turkey mince doesn't get nearly enough airtime in my opinion – it's affordable, packed with protein and simple to cook. It works particularly well with this tasty sticky, barbecue-style sauce. Put the pan in the middle of the table and let everyone help themselves.

1. Heat the oil in a large, deep frying pan over a high heat. Add the turkey and cook, stirring to break up the mince with a wooden spoon, for 10 minutes, until starting to brown.

2. Add the onion, oregano, cumin, paprika, vinegar, brown sugar, tomato purée, black beans and water. Season with salt and pepper. Give everything a good stir and cook for 5 minutes, until the sauce is very thick, and the turkey is cooked through.

3. Serve the turkey with the tortilla wraps, avocado, soured cream and lime wedges on the table and let everyone assemble their own taco.

SERVES 4

1 tbsp olive oil
500g turkey mince
1 onion, peeled and chopped
1 tsp dried oregano
2 tsp ground cumin
2 tsp paprika
1 tbsp white wine vinegar
1 tbsp soft dark brown sugar
3 tbsp tomato purée
1 x 400g tin black beans, drained and rinsed
100ml water

To Serve:
8 small tortilla wraps, warmed (see Tip, below)
1 avocado, halved, stone removed, peeled and sliced
150ml soured cream
2 limes

I usually use small soft tortilla wraps for tacos – hold them with tongs and heat (very carefully) directly over a gas hob for a couple of seconds on each side until blackened in places and warmed through. You could also use crunchy taco shells, if your family prefers.

SERVE WITH
Zesty Lime Slaw on page 159.

BRILLIANT BOWLS & HEALTHY TWISTS

ZESTY LIME SLAW
p. 159

SIDES

BALSAMIC POTATOES

Good-quality balsamic vinegar is one ingredient that I do think is worth splashing out on. If you can buy a reasonable quality one, you'll be able to taste the difference.

750g new potatoes, scrubbed and cut into bite-size pieces
300g green beans, trimmed and cut in half
2 tbsp olive oil
4 tbsp balsamic vinegar
good sprinkle of sea salt

Preheat the oven to 180°C fan/200°C/Gas Mark 6. (If you're cooking these with the cod on page 162, they can go in the oven at the same time.)

Boil the new potatoes in a large pan of boiling salted water for 10 minutes, until almost cooked through.

Add the green beans to the pan and cook for a further 2 minutes, until the beans have softened, and the potatoes are just cooked, but not breaking up. Drain the beans and potatoes.

Tip them onto a baking tray and drizzle with the oil, balsamic vinegar and salt. Give the beans and potatoes a good stir (or use clean hands) to coat them in the oil mixture. Roast for 10–15 minutes, until sticky and golden.

GARLIC & HERB MASH

Meet my favourite take on mash... it's the best in my humble opinion.

1kg potatoes (I like Maris Piper), peeled and cut into 3cm chunks
100ml whole milk
150g garlic and herb cream cheese
4 spring onions, chopped very finely
sea salt and freshly ground black pepper (don't be shy, it's needed here)

Put a large saucepan of salted water on to boil. Add the potatoes and cook for 15 minutes, or until cooked through, then drain and return to the hot pan.

Add the milk, cream cheese, spring onions and plenty of salt and pepper to the pan, then mash until smooth and creamy.

ZESTY LIME SLAW

You may need to adjust the amount of honey you use, depending on the sharpness of the apples and limes. Add a little extra honey if it's too zesty for you.

6 spring onions, halved lengthways and crossways, then cut into very thin strips
¼ white cabbage, shredded
2 green apples, cored and chopped into matchsticks, or small chunks (no need to peel)

For the Yoghurt Dressing:
100g Greek yoghurt
75g mayonnaise
2 limes, juiced and zested
2 tsp runny honey
pinch of sea salt

In a large serving bowl, mix the spring onions with the cabbage and apples.

Mix the ingredients for the dressing together and spoon it over the slaw. Toss to coat everything in the dressing. Taste and add extra honey, if needed.

Make a double or triple batch of the slaw to use in sandwiches or for lunches throughout the week. It will keep in the fridge for up to 3 days.

SPEEDY SWEET POTATO FRIES

These fries are thinly cut and cooked in a high oven to reduce the cooking time – hence 'speedy'! You're welcome to cut bigger wedges, if you fancy, they will just take a little longer to cook.

1kg sweet potatoes (about 4 medium), each potato cut into 8 thin wedges
2 tbsp olive oil
1 tsp garlic granules
1 tsp sweet smoked paprika
sea salt and freshly ground black pepper

Preheat the oven to
200°C fan/220°C/Gas Mark 7.

In a large mixing bowl, add the sweet potato wedges, oil, garlic and paprika. Season with salt and pepper and toss everything together – I find using clean hands is the best way to do this.

Spread out the potato wedges in a single layer on a baking tray and cook for 25 minutes, shuffling them about after 15 minutes, until cooked through and starting to crisp on the outside.

Space the wedges out well on a baking tray to help them to cook more quickly – you can even divide them between 2 baking trays. If they are crowded together, or touching each other, they will take longer than 25 minutes to cook.

QUICK TUNA & PEA PATTIES

A fishcake without the faff, if you will – just a couple of tins of tuna and some frozen peas mixed together to make a tasty, affordable dinner.

SERVES 4

1. Mix all the patty ingredients together in a small bowl and season with salt and pepper.

2. Heat 1 tablespoon of the oil in a large frying pan over a medium heat. Dollop a large serving spoonful of the tuna mixture into the pan and flatten the top slightly, then repeat to cook 4 patties at a time. Cook for 5 minutes on each side (don't turn them before the 5 minutes as they may stick), until golden and crisp.

3. Remove the patties from the pan to a plate lined with kitchen paper and cover with foil to keep warm. Add the rest of the oil to the pan and cook the remaining patties in the same way, so you have 8 in total. Place the second batch of patties on the kitchen paper-lined plate.

4. Meanwhile, mix all the ingredients for the yoghurt dip together.

5. Serve the patties with the dip on the side.

For the Patties:
2 x 145g tins tuna chunks in brine, drained
2 tsp mint sauce (the vinegary type, not mint jelly)
1 egg
75g plain flour
200g frozen peas, defrosted (you can leave them at room temperature or use the microwave)
1 red onion, peeled and finely chopped
2 tsp garlic granules
sea salt and freshly ground black pepper
2 tbsp olive oil, for frying

For the Yoghurt Dip:
200g Greek yoghurt
1 lemon, juiced and zested
2 tsp mint sauce (the vinegary type, not mint jelly)

SERVE WITH
Speedy Sweet Potato Fries on page 159.

SPEEDY SWEET POTATO FRIES
p. 159

PARMESAN-CRUSTED COD

This is a simple way to get the whole family to eat more fish during the week; who doesn't love cod with crunchy breadcrumbs? It's worth finding panko breadcrumbs, if you can, as their light, coarse texture gives the fish an extra crisp and crunchy coating. I prefer them to the very fine type you can buy. You can't particularly taste the mustard, it's just used as an easy way to stick the breadcrumbs to the fish.

1. Preheat the oven to 180°C fan/200°C/Gas Mark 6.

2. Pat dry each cod fillet with kitchen paper, then dollop on ½ teaspoon mustard per fillet and spread evenly over the top. (You may need a little more mustard to cover the top if they are thin, wide fillets, rather than thick ones.)

3. Mix the breadcrumbs, Parmesan and oil in a shallow bowl, then season with salt and pepper. Take the cod fillets and press them mustard-side down into the breadcrumbs so they stick in a thick, even layer. Place the fish on a baking tray lined with baking paper.

4. Bake for 10–15 minutes, until the breadcrumbs are crispy, and the fish is cooked through. Serve the fish with lemon wedges and parsley, if using.

SERVES 4

4 cod fillets (about **500g** in total)
2 tsp Dijon mustard
60g dried breadcrumbs, such as panko
30g Parmesan cheese, finely grated
2 tbsp olive oil
sea salt and freshly ground black pepper
2 lemons, cut into wedges, to serve
flat-leaf parsley, finely chopped, to garnish (optional)

The cooking time for fish fillets can vary a lot depending on their thickness, which makes timing difficult to gauge. Thinner fillets are likely to take about 10 minutes, while thicker ones will need about 15 minutes – just check they are cooked through before serving.

SERVE WITH
Balsamic Potatoes on page 158.

BALSAMIC POTATOES
p. 158

CRISPY SALMON WITH PINEAPPLE SALSA

I came up with this recipe when I was scouring around for some vegetables to serve for dinner and seeing the offering in the fridge, fruit seemed more appealing. Add a tin of sweetcorn, some lime zest and a little spice and the combination works perfectly with oily salmon. Plus, put pineapple on anything and it almost guarantees that my children will eat it without complaint – excellent dinner tactic.

1. Preheat the oven to 180°C fan/200°C/Gas Mark 6.

2. Mix the oil with the Cajun seasoning and salt, then rub the spice mix over the salmon fillets – it's easiest to do this using clean hands to make sure everything is well coated. Place the fillets on a baking tray and pop in the oven for 10–15 minutes, or until cooked through.

3. Meanwhile, cook the rice according to the instructions on the pack.

4. Mix the ingredients for the salsa together in a large bowl.

5. When the salmon is cooked, fluff up the rice with a fork and pile into bowls. Top the rice with the salmon and a good spoonful of the salsa.

SERVES 4

2 tsp sunflower oil
2 tsp Cajun seasoning
pinch of sea salt
4 salmon fillets (about **500g** in total)
300g basmati rice (or **2 x 250g** microwave pouches)

For the Pineapple Salsa:
400g pineapple, chopped into chunks (I buy a tub of ready-chopped from the supermarket)
½ red onion, peeled and chopped
1 x 200g tin sweetcorn, drained
5g fresh mint, leaves chopped
3 tbsp sweet chilli sauce
1 lime, juiced and zested
pinch of sea salt

Buy a tub of fresh, peeled and ready-chopped pineapple to reduce the preparation time.

THRIFTY TIP

Tinned pineapple is usually cheaper to buy than fresh – although I have to say I prefer fresh here if possible.

BURGERS & BREAD

ZESTY LAMB PITTAS

These fragrant lamb patties are a good way to try lamb, even if you're not usually a fan. They become crispy and golden on the outside and juicy inside when cooked, and make a delicious simple dinner piled into pitta bread.

1. Preheat the oven to 200°C fan/220°C/Gas Mark 7.

2. Mix all the ingredients for the lamb patties until combined. Season with salt and pepper.

3. Shape the lamb mixture into 8 flat patties and place on a baking tray. Bake for 15 minutes, until starting to brown all over and cooked through.

4. While the lamb is cooking, toast the pitta breads, then cut in half. Stuff the lettuce and cucumber into the toasted pitta breads and a dollop of hummus in each, and top with the lamb patties.

SERVES 4

For the Patties:
500g lean lamb mince
3 tsp ground cumin
2 tsp ground coriander
2 tsp garlic granules
1 lemon, zested
sea salt and freshly ground
    black pepper

To Serve:
4 large pitta breads
1 head of lettuce, washed and
    leaves separated
½ large cucumber, thinly sliced
200g hummus

Use beef mince instead of lamb,
if you prefer.

SERVE WITH
Roasted Aubergine Salad on page 172.

ROASTED
AUBERGINE
SALAD
p. 172

SLOPPY JOE SANDWICHES

I blame my affection for retro American-style recipes on the fact that one of my first-ever recipe books was an American kids' cookery book. The mince filling with its sticky, sweet and savoury sauce means this sandwich gets a thumbs up from adults and kids – they really are worth the mess it takes to eat them, I promise.

1. Heat the oil in a large, deep frying pan over a medium heat. Add the mince and cook for 10 minutes, stirring with a wooden spoon to break up the meat, until browned all over.

2. Add the green peppers, chopped tomatoes, mustard, sugar, ketchup and Worcestershire sauce. Season with salt and pepper, give everything a good stir, and cook over a low heat for about 10 minutes, until the sauce is very thick, and the mince is cooked through.

3. Just before the sauce is ready, toast the buns under a hot grill. Keep an eye on them as they can easily burn.

4. When the sauce is ready, pile it onto the bottom half of each toasted bun, top with the cheese slices and pop back under the grill for 30 seconds to melt the cheese. Top each one with the bun top and serve immediately.

SERVES 4

1 tsp sunflower oil
500g lean beef mince
2 green peppers, deseeded and cut into very small cubes
1 x 400g tin chopped tomatoes
2 tsp American mustard
2 tsp light brown soft sugar
2 tbsp tomato ketchup
2 tbsp Worcestershire sauce
sea salt and freshly ground black pepper

To Serve:
4 burger buns, such as brioche, split in half and toasted
4 slices of mature Cheddar cheese

★

I love a pickle here, but I've left it out of the recipe as I know that they aren't to everyone's taste but do add pickles if you like.

SERVE WITH
Cheesy Corn on page 172.

CHEESY CORN
p. 172

SIDES

CHEESY CORN

This recipe is inspired by the Mexican corn street food, elote. Here, I've used chilli sauce instead of chilli powder to avoid scaring off children but do try the real thing if you ever get the chance – grilled over fire, it's incredible.

4 corn on the cob
4 tsp (20g) mayonnaise
2 tsp chilli sauce
25g Parmesan cheese, grated
1 lime, cut in half

Preheat the grill to high.

Cook the corn under the grill for about 10 minutes, turning regularly (they will start to slightly blacken).

Meanwhile, mix the mayonnaise and chilli sauce in a small bowl. Put the Parmesan in a large shallow bowl.

When cooked, drain the corn and brush the cobs all over with the mayo mixture (or roll them in it). Next, roll the corn in the grated Parmesan so the chilli mayo acts as a sort of 'glue'.

Squeeze over the lime juice and serve immediately.

ROASTED AUBERGINE SALAD

Roasting is a good way to cook aubergines for even the most ardent vegetable hater.

2 large aubergines, cut into 2cm cubes
1 tbsp olive oil
2 tsp sweet smoked paprika
200g Greek yoghurt
5g fresh mint, leaves chopped
1 lemon, juiced
1 tsp sea salt

Preheat the oven to 200°C fan/220°C/Gas Mark 7 (if you'r serving this with the lamb pittas on page 168, it will be on already).

Put the aubergines on a baking tray and drizzle with the oil and smoked paprika, then toss to make sure everything is combined.

Roast for 15 minutes (if you are making this with the Zesty Lamb Pittas, everything can go in the oven together), until tender and browned in places.

Remove from the oven and mix the aubergines with the yoghurt, mint, lemon juice and salt. Stir well and serve.

COWBOY CAVIAR

Originally served up in the 1940s by a New York chef working in Texas, this salad was a nod to what she thought cowboys were feasting on instead of regular caviar. Cowboy, or not, you must try it.

A take on this has been a viral recipe on TikTok recently and I promise it's as good as the hype.

1 red pepper, deseeded and chopped into 1cm cubes
6 spring onions, finely chopped
1 x 200g tin sweetcorn, drained
200g fresh tomato salsa
(from the supermarket dips aisle)
1 x 400g tin black beans, drained
2 limes, juiced and zested
jalapeños from a jar, to taste

Mix the salad ingredients together in a bowl and serve.

WEDGE SALAD

I'm not sure you could find a salad leaf more boring to eat than the poor old iceberg, but cutting it into wedges redeems it here – and covering it in bacon, of course, too. A traditional American steakhouse wedge salad comes with a blue cheese dressing. I've left it out here as it's not to everyone's taste, but please do crumble 75g of your favourite blue cheese into the dressing, if it's your thing.

100g smoked bacon lardons
1 large iceberg lettuce
150g cherry tomatoes, chopped into small pieces

For the Dressing:
60g Greek yoghurt
60g mayonnaise
2 lemons, juiced
2 tsp garlic granules
2 tsp onion powder

Cook the bacon pieces in a small dry frying pan over a medium heat for 5–10 minutes, until very crisp and golden. Drain on a plate lined with kitchen paper and set aside.

Meanwhile, remove the outer leaves of the lettuce and cut it into quarters, so you end up with 4 big wedges.

Mix all the ingredients for the dressing together in a small bowl, adding enough water to make it a pourable consistency.

Place the lettuce wedges on a serving plate, drizzle over the dressing and sprinkle with the chopped tomatoes and bacon pieces.

BARBECUE CHICKEN BURGERS

You could use a shop-bought barbecue sauce here to similar effect, but I do like to make my own version as I know exactly what's going into it and can also tweak the flavours slightly if I fancy. A digital meat thermometer is useful here to make sure that the chicken breasts are cooked through. In the past, I've tended to overcook them 'just in case' but using a thermometer avoids the guesswork.

1. Preheat the oven to 200°C fan/220°C/Gas Mark 7.

2. Mix the ingredients for the BBQ sauce in a small bowl.

3. Put the chicken in a large bowl and spoon over the sauce. Turn to coat the chicken in the sauce (there may be some sauce left in the bottom of the bowl, set this aside).

4. Put the chicken on a lined baking tray and bake for 25 minutes in total.

5. After the chicken has been in the oven for 15 minutes, place the bacon rashers next to it on the tray. At the same time, turn the chicken over and spoon any remaining sauce on top. Cook the bacon with the chicken for the remaining 10 minutes.

6. Two minutes before the chicken and bacon are ready, sit a cheese slice on top of the chicken. Pop the tray back into the oven to finish cooking the chicken and for the cheese to melt.

7. Check that the chicken is cooked all the way through and serve the chicken burgers in the buns, adding lettuce and bacon.

SERVES 4

4 skinless, boneless chicken breasts (about **600g** in total)
8 streaky bacon rashers
4 slices of Cheddar cheese

For the BBQ Sauce:
4 tbsp tomato ketchup
2 tbsp soft dark brown sugar
2 tsp Dijon mustard
2 tsp runny honey
1 tsp garlic granules
1 tsp sweet smoked paprika
sea salt and freshly ground black pepper

To Serve:
4 burger buns, split in half and toasted, if you like
lettuce leaves

SERVE WITH
Cowboy Caviar on page 173.

COWBOY CAVIAR →
p. 173

SPEEDY SMASH BURGERS

These burgers are all about keeping it simple, but with one nifty trick. I roll each one into a ball, pop it into a hot pan, then squash it flat. Doing this instead of shaping the mixture into patties gives the burgers the most satisfying crunchy textured surface. Top them with my homemade burger sauce and you have a fast-food feast.

1. Mix all the ingredients for the burger sauce in a small bowl and set aside.

2. Heat the oil in a large frying pan (preferably one with a lid) over a medium-high heat.

3. Mix the mince, onion powder, garlic granules and ketchup in a mixing bowl. Season with salt and pepper and shape into 4 balls – it's easiest to do this with your hands, but don't squash them yet.

4. Get prepared with a heavy fish slice or spatula in hand (see tip, below right). Put the meatballs into the very hot pan and after about 30 seconds, squash them into a flat burger shape by pressing down with the fish slice or spatula.

5. Cook the burgers for 4 minutes on each side, until crisp and golden. About 1 minute before they are ready, top each burger with a cheese slice (if your pan has a lid pop it on at this point) and cook until the cheese starts to melt.

6. Serve the burgers in the toasted buns, topped with the sauce and lettuce.

1 tbsp sunflower oil
500g lean beef mince
1 tsp onion powder
1 tsp garlic granules
2 tsp tomato ketchup
4 cheese slices
sea salt and freshly ground
    black pepper

For the Burger Sauce:
3 tbsp (45g) mayonnaise
3 tbsp American mustard
2 tbsp tomato ketchup
2 gherkins, finely diced (optional)

To Serve:
4 burger buns, such as brioche,
    split in half and toasted
lettuce leaves (optional)

If you don't have a sturdy fish slice or spatula, squash the burgers with the bottom of a small saucepan. This is also excellent for working off any anger! Place the burger balls in the very hot pan, place a small square of baking paper on top of each one and press down firmly with the bottom of the pan to your desired burger thickness.

SERVE WITH
Wedge Salad on page 173.

WEDGE SALAD
p. 173

LOADED SAUSAGE SUBS

This is inspired by the meaty sausage subs served in Italian delis in New York. Stuffed with pieces of sausage, sweet fried onions and peppers, this sub makes a messy but delicious hand-held dinner. Enjoy... and make sure you have lots of napkins to hand.

1. Preheat the oven to 200°C fan/220°C/Gas Mark 7.

2. Heat the oil in a large, deep frying pan over a medium heat. Add the sausages and fry for 5 minutes, turning occasionally, until they start to colour.

3. Using scissors, snip each sausage into 3 pieces (no need to take them out of the pan). Add the onion and red pepper to the pan and fry for a further 5 minutes, until the vegetables have softened.

4. Meanwhile, bake the rolls in the oven for 5 minutes, or until cooked, then set aside.

5. Add the chopped tomatoes, oregano and balsamic vinegar to the sausage mixture. Season with salt and pepper, give everything a good stir and cook over a medium-low heat for about 10 minutes, stirring occasionally, until the sausages are cooked through and the sauce has thickened.

6. Split the rolls in half (so each half is still joined but can be opened), sit them in a roasting tin and pile the sausage mixture inside each one. Top with the mozzarella and pop into the oven for 5 minutes, until the mozzarella melts.

SERVES 4

1 tbsp olive oil
400g pork sausages
   (about 6 in total)
1 onion, peeled and thinly sliced
1 red pepper, deseeded and
   cut into strips
4 part-baked bread rolls
1 x 400g tin chopped tomatoes
1 tsp dried oregano
2 tbsp balsamic vinegar
100g grated mozzarella cheese
sea salt and freshly ground
   black pepper

I find the part-baked 'bake at home' bread rolls work well here as they don't go too soft when topped with the saucy sausages, but you can use freshly baked rolls, if you prefer.

THRIFTY TIP

This is perfect for using up small bits of leftover cheese in place of mozzarella – use whatever you have available.

SERVE WITH
Pesto Potato Salad on page 182.

BURGERS & BREAD

PESTO POTATO SALAD

p. 182

PORK & APPLE BURGERS

These are just what a good burger should be – simple but delicious. The trick is to add some grated apple to help them keep their shape and stay juicy. There's no need to peel the apples, in fact I think the texture is better if you don't. I suggest serving the burgers with my Rainbow Coleslaw; its nutty crunch adds a delicious contrast to the burgers.

1. In a large mixing bowl, mix the pork, sage and apple until combined – it's easiest to do this with your hands. Season with salt and pepper, then shape into 4 patties.

2. Heat the oil in a large frying pan over a medium heat. Add the burgers and cook for 13–15 minutes, flipping them halfway through, until golden on the outside and cooked through.

3. Serve the burgers in the toasted buns with your choice of toppings piled on top.

SERVES 4

500g pork mince
1 tsp dried sage
1 eating apple, grated
    (no need to peel)
2 tbsp sunflower oil
sea salt and freshly ground
    black pepper

To serve:
4 burger buns, such as brioche,
    split in half, toasted
avocado slices
tomato slices
lettuce leaves

SERVE WITH
Rainbow Coleslaw on page 183.

RAINBOW COLESLAW
p. 183

SIDES

PESTO POTATO SALAD

Use a jar of pesto, that family faithful, to elevate a standard potato salad. Serve with the sausage subs or it also makes a super side dish for a picnic or barbecue.

750g new potatoes, scrubbed and halved if large
300g green beans, trimmed and cut in half

For the Pesto Dressing:
100g Greek yoghurt
75g mayonnaise
2 tbsp green pesto
1 lemon, juiced and zested
50g pine nuts (optional, but they add a lovely crunch)

Cook the potatoes in boiling salted water for 10–13 minutes, or until they are almost cooked. Add the green beans and cook for a further 3–5 minutes, until tender. Drain the potatoes and beans and tip them into a serving bowl.

Mix all the ingredients for the pesto dressing together. Spoon it over the potatoes and beans and turn to coat them in the dressing.

SPICED CAULIFLOWER SALAD

Roasting cauliflower gives our friend the pale cauli colour and texture that makes it incredibly moreish.

1 cauliflower (about **500g**), leaves removed and cut into small florets
2 tbsp sunflower oil
3 tsp ground cumin
3 tsp garam masala
pinch of sea salt

For the Dressing:
150g natural yoghurt
2 tsp mint sauce (the vinegary type, not jelly)

Preheat the oven to 200°C fan/220°C/Gas Mark 7. (If you are cooking the Chicken Tikka-style Naan Burgers on page 184 it will be on anyway and you can cook everything at the same time.)

Put the cauliflower into a large bowl and toss with the oil, cumin, garam masala and salt until the florets are coated all over. Roast for 25 minutes, until cooked through and the florets are just starting to blacken at the edges.

Meanwhile, mix all the ingredients for the dressing together.

Serve the cauliflower warm, drizzled with the dressing.

CRUNCHY PEANUT SALAD

This is the ultimate 'doesn't-taste-like-salad' salad – perfect for lettuce dodgers like me. You can make it a few hours ahead of serving and add the dressing at the last minute. It goes so well with barbecue food, grilled meat or fish, or you could even enjoy eating a bowl of it as a meal in itself.

2 red peppers, deseeded and cut into 2cm pieces
6 spring onions, cut into small pieces
1 cucumber, cut into small pieces
1 ripe mango, peeled, stone removed and cut into small pieces
50g roasted peanuts, finely chopped, to serve

For the Peanut Dressing:
50g crunchy peanut butter
2 tbsp soy sauce
1 tbsp sweet chilli sauce
1 tbsp runny honey
2 tbsp water (see note below)
2 limes, juiced and zested

Mix all the dressing ingredients together with 2 tablespoons water until smooth using a balloon whisk or fork – it will look split at first but keep going and it will come good.

Put the red peppers, spring onions, cucumber and mango in a serving bowl. Spoon the dressing over and gently turn until combined. Sprinkle with the peanuts before serving.

Natural peanut butter is a lot more runny than regular so you may need less water if you're using a natural brand.

RAINBOW COLESLAW

Make a double, or triple, batch of this slaw to use in sandwiches or for lunches throughout the week. Squeeze any liquid out of the grated carrots before adding to the mixture, and the slaw will keep in the fridge for up to 3 days without going watery.

½ large red onion, peeled and cut into thin slices
¼ red cabbage, shredded
2 carrots, peeled and coarsely grated
50g walnuts, roughly chopped, to serve

For the Yogurt Dressing:
100g Greek yoghurt
75g mayonnaise
1 tsp wholegrain mustard

In a large serving bowl, mix the onion with the cabbage and carrots.

Mix all the ingredients for the dressing together and spoon it over the slaw. Toss to coat the vegetables in the dressing.

Serve the slaw topped with the walnuts.

CHICKEN TIKKA-STYLE NAAN BURGERS

This is a quick and simple way to spice up a pack of chicken breasts for a weekday dinner. If you can't find tikka seasoning, use another mild type of curry powder to suit your own tastes. You don't have to bother with flattening the chicken breasts, if you prefer not to, but it does help to cook them more quickly and evenly.

1. Preheat the oven to 200°C fan/220°C/Gas Mark 7.

2. Place one of the chicken breasts between 2 sheets of baking paper, then bash with the end of a rolling pin or the base of saucepan to flatten the thickest part so the breast is an even thickness. Repeat with all 4 chicken breasts.

3. Put the chicken breasts in a dish. Mix the oil, tikka seasoning and salt, then add to the chicken and turn until coated in the spice oil. Place the chicken on a baking tray lined with baking paper.

4. Bake the chicken for 18–20 minutes, or until cooked through (this will vary depending on the thickness and size of the chicken breasts – a meat thermometer is useful here if you have one).

5. Place the naan breads in the oven 5 minutes before the end of the chicken cooking time to warm through.

6. Meanwhile, mix all the ingredients for the dressing together in a small bowl.

7. To serve, split the warm naan breads along one edge to create a pocket. Pile the mango chutney, lettuce, red onion and dressing into each naan bread, then add the cooked chicken.

SERVES 4

4 skinless, boneless chicken breasts
    (about **600g** in total)
2 tsp sunflower oil
6 tsp tikka seasoning
½ tsp sea salt
4 mini naan breads

For the Dressing:
½ cucumber, cut into small cubes
100g natural yoghurt
2 tsp mint sauce (the vinegary
    type, not mint jelly)

To Serve:
80g mango chutney
1 head of lettuce
    (I like romaine), shredded
1 red onion, peeled and cut into rings

Fresh naan bread from the supermarket bakery section tends to be softer and easier to split than the long-life ones sold in packets. Briefly holding the naan breads under a running tap before baking can help soften them – they should be damp and not too wet.

SERVE WITH
Spiced Cauliflower Salad on page 182.

SPICED
CAULIFLOWER SALAD
p. 182

STICKY PEANUT STRIPS

Supermarket packs of chicken mini fillets are very handy here, but you could cut up chicken breasts, if you prefer. The simple marinade transforms the strips of chicken into something altogether more impressive – nutty, zesty and full of flavour. Leftovers make an excellent lunch too.

1. Preheat the oven to 180°C fan/200°C/Gas Mark 6.

2. Put the chicken into a large bowl. Mix the marinade ingredients together, add to the bowl and stir until the chicken is coated in the marinade. Cover and leave to marinate in the fridge for 10 minutes.

3. Place the chicken pieces on a baking tray lined with baking paper and roast for 10 minutes, turning halfway, until cooked through.

4. Meanwhile, mix all the ingredients together for the dressing.

5. Five minutes before the chicken is ready, wrap the tortillas in a foil parcel and warm in the oven. Serve the tortillas topped with the chicken and drizzle with the dressing.

600g mini chicken fillets
4 small tortilla wraps

For the Marinade:
50g smooth peanut butter
1 tbsp sunflower oil
1 tbsp soy sauce
2 tsp garlic granules
2 tsp curry powder
1 lime, juiced and zested

For the Dressing:
100g Greek yoghurt
1 lime, juiced and zested
2 tsp runny honey
½ tsp sea salt

SERVE WITH
Crunchy Peanut Salad on page 183.

CRUNCHY PEANUT SALAD
p. 183

WEEKEND TREATS

IVY'S CHEESE SCONES

Ivy was my maternal grandmother, a powerhouse of an East End lady, who was a cook in the 1930s, and her scones were legendary. She gave me this recipe when I was 10 years old, scribbled on a scrap of paper, and I've been using it ever since. Don't be fearful of making scones, once you get the knack, they are one of the quickest and most satisfying bakes I know.

1. Preheat the oven as high as it will go, usually 220°C fan/240°C/Gas Mark 9. Line a baking sheet with baking paper.

2. Put the flour, baking powder, mustard powder and salt into a mixing bowl.

3. Add the butter and rub it in with your hands (you loosely lift some of the butter with the flour mixture and rub it between the tips of your thumb and fingers to break up the butter into smaller pieces) until it looks like lumpy sand. It will take about 5 minutes.

4. Stir in half of the grated cheese, then add the milk and use your hands to gently bring it all together into a ball of dough.

5. Lightly dust the worktop and a rolling pin with flour. Roll out or pat the dough with your hands to slightly flatten to about 2.5cm–3cm thick. Cut out 8 round circles using a 7cm round cutter or upturned glass.

6. Pop the scones onto the lined baking sheet, brush the tops with beaten egg and sprinkle over the remaining cheese. Bake for 10 minutes, or until risen and golden.

MAKES 8 BIG SCONES

500g plain flour, plus extra for rolling
3 tsp baking powder
1 tsp English mustard powder
1 tsp sea salt
80g butter, straight from the fridge, cut into chunks
200g mature Cheddar cheese, coarsely grated
300ml whole milk
1 egg, beaten

If you don't have mustard powder replace it with ½ teaspoon cayenne pepper or paprika.

Scones are best served fresh on the day you bake them. If you want to serve them the next day, toast and fill with bacon for breakfast. (They also freeze well, but why deny yourself that bacon-filled joy.)

OATMEAL CHUNK COOKIES

(V)

These are a spin on my classic oatmeal cookie recipe. Given that they are one of the most popular weekend bakes in my house, I feel I'd be letting you down if I didn't include a version here. There's something about putting oats in a cookie that makes them feel vaguely wholesome, and chocolate chunks improve everything – right?

1. Preheat the oven to 200°C fan/220°C/Gas Mark 7. Line 2 baking sheets with baking paper (if you only have 1 baking sheet, you can bake them in 2 batches).

2. In a mixing bowl, beat the butter and sugar together with an electric hand whisk or wooden spoon until light and fluffy. Beat in the egg and vanilla extract until well combined.

3. Fold in the remaining dry ingredients and stir well. Bring everything together into a ball of dough with clean hands.

4. Divide the dough into 12 equal-sized balls and place spaced out on the lined baking sheets so they have room to spread. Bake for 12–14 minutes, until just starting to brown.

5. Leave the cookies to cool on the baking sheet until they are firm enough to handle.

MAKES 12

100g unsalted butter, at room temperature
150g light brown soft sugar
1 egg
1 tsp vanilla extract
100g plain flour
½ tsp ground cinnamon
½ tsp baking powder
½ tsp sea salt
125g rolled oats
75g milk or plain chocolate, cut into chunks

Rolled porridge oats work best – don't use instant, quick-cook oats or the cookies will spread too much.

I use a small ice cream scoop to measure out the dough into even-sized balls.

CHOCOLATE BROWNIE COOKIES

These cookies should be soft and gooey, just like a good brownie – don't over-bake them, or they will be too crunchy. They make an excellent 'bread' for an ice-cream sandwich too.

1. Preheat the oven to 180°C fan/200°C/Gas Mark 6. Line 2 baking sheets with baking paper (if you only have 1 baking sheet, you can bake them in 2 batches).

2. Mix all the ingredients together in a large mixing bowl with an electric hand whisk or wooden spoon. (Reserve a handful of the chocolate chips to decorate the cookies.)

3. Using a dessert spoon, place 12 even-sized dollops of the cookie mixture onto the lined baking sheets. Make sure they are evenly spaced apart to allow space for spreading. Press the saved chocolate chips into the tops of the cookies.

4. Bake the cookies for 13–15 minutes, or until the outsides are just starting to crisp. Don't over-cook them – they will still be soft but will firm up as they cool.

5. Leave to cool on the baking sheets before tucking in.

Make 24 small cookies, if you prefer.

MAKES 12

150g unsalted butter, softened
75g caster sugar
75g soft dark brown sugar
1 egg
200g plain flour
20g cocoa powder
½ tsp sea salt
1 tsp baking powder
100g white chocolate chips
100g plain chocolate chips

THRIFTY TIP

You can replace the chocolate chips with any chopped leftover chocolate you may have (leftover chocolate – what's that?).

BISCUIT TIN TIFFIN

In the words of writer, Caitlin Moran, 'Always remember that nine times out of ten, you probably aren't having a full-on nervous breakdown – you just need a cup of tea and a biscuit. You'd be amazed how easily and repeatedly you can confuse the two. Get a big biscuit tin.' Heeding these wise words, I like to keep a ready and varied supply of biscuits available in case of an emergency. This is the recipe for when the last few in those packets no longer quite fulfil the required crunch – they are upcycled into something, dare I say it, even better. The hands-on time for these is about 5 minutes, so I hope you can forgive the chilling time needed.

1. Line a 20cm square baking tin with baking paper.

2. Put the butter, 200g of the milk chocolate, the plain chocolate and golden syrup into a large microwaveable bowl. Microwave in 30-second blasts, stirring very well between each stint – even if it looks like it doesn't need to be stirred. (If you prefer, you can put everything into a heatproof bowl set over a pan of simmering water on the hob. Don't let the bottom of the bowl touch the water and stir occasionally until the chocolate melts.)

3. When the chocolate mixture is melted and smooth, stir in the biscuits and Brazil nuts until they are totally coated. (I like to save some biscuit crumbs to sprinkle over at the end.)

4. Spoon the mixture into the lined baking tin – you'll need to press it down firmly with the back of a spoon to an even thickness.

5. Melt the remaining milk chocolate in the same way, as above, then pour it over the top of the biscuit mix to cover. Sprinkle with the saved biscuit crumbs.

6. Chill in the fridge for 2 hours or overnight, until set. Cut into squares to serve.

150g unsalted butter
350g milk chocolate, broken into pieces
200g plain chocolate (minimum 55–70% cocoa solids), broken into pieces
4 tbsp golden syrup
400g biscuits, broken into chunks
50g Brazil nuts, chopped into big chunks (or the same weight of raisins, if you prefer)

It took me years to master melting chocolate in the microwave – the trick is to mix it for almost as long as you heat it each time. This helps to stop the chocolate burning and allows it to melt evenly.

THRIFTY TIP

This is perfect for using up past-their-best biscuits lingering in the bottom of the tin. I find that the more random the combination, the better – custard creams and chocolate fingers in one bite is a total treat.

CHEAT'S DANISH PASTRIES

Who wouldn't fancy a flaky, bakery-style pastry fresh from the oven on a weekend morning? This shortcut version will make your brunch dreams come true – a sheet of puff pastry and some jam when paired together using a nifty fold, look and taste altogether more impressive than the very minimal effort involved. Be careful to let them cool a little before eating as the jam will be scorching hot when they come out of the oven.

1. Preheat the oven to 200°C fan/220°C/Gas Mark 7. Line a baking sheet with baking paper.

2. Unroll the sheet of puff pastry and cut it into 8 squares. Place a dollop of jam in the middle of each square, top with the raspberries. Bring the four corners of the pastry together to meet in the middle over the top of the jam.

3. Use a little of the beaten egg to seal the pastry join if you need to. Repeat to make 8 in total and place on the lined baking sheet.

4. Brush the pastries with the remaining egg and bake for 15–20 minutes, until golden and crisp – no soggy bottoms allowed.

5. Meanwhile, mix the icing sugar with 1 tablespoon water in a bowl until it forms a thick icing.

6. Remove the pastries from the oven. Leave to cool on a wire rack, then drizzle with the icing.

MAKES 8

375g ready-rolled puff pastry from the fridge (leave to come to room temperature for 15 minutes)
300g jam of choice
200g raspberries
1 egg, beaten
75g icing sugar, sifted

If you drizzle the icing on when the pastries are warm, it will sink in a little (but still be delicious).

THRIFTY TIP
Ready-rolled puff pastry normally comes on a sheet of baking paper, which you can reuse to line the baking sheet.

STRAWBERRY SHORTCAKES

If you're in the market for a speedy bake these large shortcakes – a take on the sweet scone – are your friend. Piled high with cream and strawberries – a plate of these is a thing of beauty.

MAKES 4 LARGE

250g plain flour, plus extra for rolling
1½ tsp baking powder
1 tsp caster sugar
40g unsalted butter, straight from the fridge, cut into chunks
150ml whole milk
1 egg, lightly beaten

To Serve:
125ml double cream
1 tsp vanilla extract
1 tbsp icing sugar
50g strawberry jam
75g strawberries (about 6), sliced

1. Preheat the oven as high as it will go, usually 220°C fan/240°C/Gas Mark 9. Line a baking sheet with baking paper.

2. Mix the flour, baking powder and caster sugar in a large mixing bowl.

3. Add the butter and rub it in with your hands (you loosely lift some of the butter with the flour mixture and rub it between the tips of your thumb and fingers to break up the butter into smaller pieces) until it looks like lumpy sand. It will take about 5 minutes.

4. Stir in the milk and use your hands to gently bring it all together into a ball of dough.

5. Lightly dust the worktop and a rolling pin with flour. Roll out or pat the dough with your hands to slightly flatten to about 2.5cm–3cm thick. Cut out 8 round circles using a 7cm round cutter or upturned glass.

6. Pop them onto the lined baking sheet and brush the tops with beaten egg. Bake for 10 minutes, or until risen and golden. Leave to cool on a wire rack.

7. Meanwhile, in a large mixing bowl, whisk the double cream, vanilla extract and icing sugar until it forms soft peaks (something like the consistency of soft-serve ice cream.) If you have an electric whisk, use it to save time and save yourself getting arm ache!

8. To serve, cut the shortcakes in half, then dollop on the strawberry jam, whipped cream and sliced strawberries.

These are best served on the day you bake them. Any leftover unfilled shortcakes freeze well – open freeze on a baking sheet, then transfer to a freezer-proof container.

Fill just an hour or two before serving as once filled, the shortcakes can go quite soft.

This recipe makes 4 big shortcakes, but feel free to make double the quantity.

SALTED PRETZEL FUDGE

This isn't technically real fudge as the method is slightly different, but it's every bit as good in my opinion. Keep a block in the fridge – although you'll find it's almost impossible to walk past it, without sneaking a cube.

1. Line a 20cm square baking tin with baking paper.

2. Put the milk chocolate and condensed milk into a large microwaveable bowl. Microwave for 30 seconds, then beat well – repeat once or twice until the mixture is very thick and smooth.

3. Mix in the pretzel pieces and pour into the lined baking tin. Smooth and level the mixture, then press the remaining pretzels on top.

4. Chill overnight in the fridge, then cut into small pieces and keep in the fridge until ready to serve.

MAKES ABOUT 36 PIECES

400g milk chocolate
1 x 397g tin condensed milk
100g pretzels, broken into pieces, plus an extra **25g** to decorate

PEANUT BUTTER & JELLY COOKIES

Just four ingredients are used to make these super easy, tea-time treats, which are accidentally also gluten free and dairy free. I've made large cookies, but you can make smaller ones if you prefer – but where's the fun in that!

1. Preheat the oven to 180°C fan/200°C/Gas Mark 6. Line a baking sheet with baking paper.

2. Mix the peanut butter, sugar and egg in a large mixing bowl with a wooden spoon until combined.

3. Using 2 dessert spoons, place 8 even-sized rough dollops of the cookie mixture onto the lined baking sheet. Make sure they are evenly spaced apart to allow space for spreading.

4. Using your thumb, make an indent in the centre of each cookie and spoon a little jam in the hole – don't overfill or it will dribble out.

5. Bake the cookies for 15 minutes, or until turning golden – they will spread out to palm size during baking. (They will still be very soft at this point but will firm up as they cool.) Take care as the jam will be very hot.

6. Leave to cool on the baking sheet before tucking in.

MAKES 8 BIG COOKIES

250g smooth sugar-free peanut butter
200g caster sugar
1 egg
50g jam of choice (strawberry or raspberry work well)

Try not to handle the cookie too much as it can become greasy – it's best to use dessert spoons to dollop the balls of dough onto the baking sheet.

THRIFTY TIP

This is a great way to use up those nearly finished jars of jam lingering in the fridge.

LEMON & RASPBERRY MUFFINS

The sight of these happy looking little muffins makes me feel like I should be sitting down with a cup of tea in a china cup and giving them attention they deserve. An excellent plan for a Sunday afternoon if you ask me. They're also ideal for packed lunches and cake-shaped rewards.

1. **Preheat the oven to 180°C fan/200°C/Gas Mark 6. Line a muffin tray with 12 small muffin cases or 8 large ones.**

2. **Beat the butter and sugar in a mixing bowl with an electric hand whisk or wooden spoon until light and fluffy.**

3. **Add the eggs, flour and the lemon zest and beat until well combined. Gently fold in the raspberries (try not to break them up too much).**

4. **Divide the cake batter evenly between the muffin cases. Bake for 20–25 minutes if making large muffins or 15–20 minutes if making small ones, until risen, golden and cooked through when you poke a skewer into the middle of a muffin. Leave the muffins to cool in the tray.**

5. **While the muffins are cooling, make the drizzle. Mix the lemon juice with the sugar and spoon it over the muffins as they cool.**

depending on the size of the muffin cases

MAKES 8–12

150g unsalted butter, at room temperature
150g caster sugar
3 eggs
150g self-raising flour
2 lemons, zested
150g raspberries

To Drizzle:
50ml lemon juice (from the zested lemons)
25g caster sugar

TOFFEE POPCORN ROCKY ROAD

Chocolatey, chewy and so moreish... this rocky road is made with popcorn instead of the more usual biscuits for a lighter texture. It makes a brilliant bake sale recipe if the need arises. It's quick to make but does need some time to chill.

1. Line a 20cm square baking tin with baking paper.

2. Put the butter, milk chocolate, plain chocolate and golden syrup into a large microwaveable bowl.

3. Microwave in 30 second blasts, stirring well between each stint – even if it looks like it doesn't need to be stirred. (If you prefer, you can put everything into a heatproof bowl set over a pan of simmering water on the hob. Don't let the bottom of the bowl touch the water and stir occasionally until the chocolate melts.)

4. When the mixture is melted and smooth, add the marshmallows and popcorn. Mix everything together well – this will take a few minutes (it's a good job for children to do as it keeps them amused for a while).

5. Spoon the mixture into the lined baking tin – you'll need to press it down firmly with the back of a spoon to fit it all in.

6. Melt the white chocolate in the same way, as above, then drizzle it over the top. Chill in the fridge for 2 hours or overnight, until set. Cut into 16 squares to serve.

MAKES 16

150g unsalted butter
200g milk chocolate, broken into pieces
200g plain chocolate (minimum 55–70% cocoa solids), broken into pieces
4 tbsp golden syrup
150g mini marshmallows
120g toffee popcorn
100g white chocolate, broken into pieces

It took me years to master melting chocolate in the microwave – the trick is to mix it for almost as long as you heat it each time. This helps to stop the chocolate burning and allows it melt evenly.

THRIFTY TIP

You can use up any leftover chocolate for this recipe as long as it's the same weight.

NUTRITIONAL INFORMATION

Please use the nutritional information here as an approximate guide only. If you need exact measurements please confirm using your own branded ingredients. All measurements are per serving (as per the recipe page).

WEEKEND BREAKFASTS

SWEETCORN FETA FRITTERS
(Per Serving)

Kcals: 604
Protein: 27.3g
Carbs: 61.3g
Sugar: 16.2g
Fat: 25.9g
Saturated fat: 9.1g
Fibre: 7.6g
Salt: 1.89g

30

VERY BERRY BAKED OATS
(Per Serving)

Kcals: 351
Protein: 15.8g
Carbs: 40.1g
Sugar: 15.3g
Fat: 12.7g
Saturated fat: 2.8g
Fibre: 7.0g
Salt: 0.36g

32

34

PEACH COBBLER BAKED OATS
(Per Serving)

Kcals: 316
Protein: 14.4g
Carbs: 41.1g
Sugar: 16.0g
Fat: 9.2g
Saturated fat: 2.6g
Fibre: 5.7g
Salt: 0.6g

35

APPLE PIE BAKED OATS
(Per Serving)

Kcals: 373
Protein: 14.6g
Carbs: 53.3g
Sugar: 28.5g
Fat: 10.0g
Saturated fat: 2.9g
Fibre: 6.0g
Salt: 0.58g

SAVOURY STUFFED CROISSANTS
(Per Serving)

Kcals: 401
Protein: 19.3g
Carbs: 25.7g
Sugar: 4.9g
Fat: 23.9g
Saturated fat: 12.8g
Fibre: 2.3g
Salt: 1.85g

36

BACON, EGG & CHEESE MUFFINS
(Per Serving)

Kcals: 607
Protein: 37.2g
Carbs: 29.2g
Sugar: 2.5g
Fat: 37.5g
Saturated fat: 16.8g
Fibre: 1.9g
Salt: 3.87g

38

FULL ENGLISH BAKE
(Per Serving)

Kcals: 541
Protein: 31.1g
Carbs: 11.3g
Sugar: 5.1g
Fat: 40.4g
Saturated fat: 13.8g
Fibre: 3.8g
Salt: 2.43g

40

SKY-HIGH BLUEBERRY PANCAKES
(Per Serving)

Kcals: 482
Protein: 13.5g
Carbs: 79.7g
Sugar: 24.4g
Fat: 11.2g
Saturated fat: 2.6g
Fibre: 4.1g
Salt: 2.71g

42

EGG MUFFIN CUPS
(Per Serving)

Kcals: 284
Protein: 25.4g
Carbs: 1.2g
Sugar: 1.2g
Fat: 19.7g
Saturated fat: 7.7g
Fibre: 0.4g
Salt: 1.41g

44

CHEESE & HAM PUFFS
(Per Serving)

Kcals: 317
Protein: 12.0g
Carbs: 17.3g
Sugar: 1.6g
Fat: 21.9g
Saturated fat: 10.6g
Fibre: 1.8g
Salt: 1.54g

46

MEAT-FREE MONDAYS

LENTIL LINGUINE
(Per Serving)

Kcals: 705
Protein: 29.7g
Carbs: 96.5g
Sugar: 21.6g
Fat: 18g
Saturated fat: 2.2g
Fibre: 18.1g
Salt: 0.19g

50

GET WELL SOON SOUP
(Per Serving)

Kcals: 294
Protein: 17.7g
Carbs: 37.8g
Sugar: 7.3g
Fat: 4.7g
Saturated fat: 0.7g
Fibre: 14.3g
Salt: 2.37g

52

CAULIFLOWER CHEESE SOUP
(Per Serving)

Kcals: 324
Protein: 19.1g
Carbs: 17.6g
Sugar: 13.4g
Fat: 18.6g
Saturated fat: 10.9g
Fibre: 4.7g
Salt: 2.82g

54

DOUBLE CHEESE GARLIC BREAD
(Per Serving)

Kcals: 538
Protein: 15.5g
Carbs: 41.4g
Sugar: 2.6g
Fat: 33.8g
Saturated fat: 20.9g
Fibre: 3.0g
Salt: 2.37g

56

PARMESAN CROUTONS
(Per Serving)

Kcals: 359
Protein: 10.6g
Carbs: 39.3g
Sugar: 3.1g
Fat: 17.2g
Saturated fat: 3.4g
Fibre: 2.5g
Salt: 1.74g

57

GREEN GOODNESS SALAD
(Per Serving)

Kcals: 213
Protein: 3.8g
Carbs: 5.7g
Sugar: 4.8g
Fat: 17.9g
Saturated fat: 3.1g
Fibre: 5.5g
Salt: 0.45g

57

FOUR-CHEESE FRITTATA
(Per Serving)

Kcals: 658
Protein: 36.2g
Carbs: 36.8g
Sugar: 8.5g
Fat: 39.1g
Saturated fat: 16.4g
Fibre: 7.2g
Salt: 1.57g

58

SMOKY HALLOUMI BEAN BAKE
(Per Serving)

Kcals: 692
Protein: 40.9g
Carbs: 50.6g
Sugar: 19.7g
Fat: 31g
Saturated fat: 19.7g
Fibre: 16.6g
Salt: 3.5g

60

CHICKPEA PEANUT BUTTER CURRY
(Per Serving)

Kcals: 754
Protein: 22.4g
Carbs: 81.4g
Sugar: 9.7g
Fat: 34.5g
Saturated fat: 18.5g
Fibre: 13.8g
Salt: 0.45g

62

CHUNKY TORTELLINI SOUP
(Per Serving)

Kcals: 403
Protein: 18.7g
Carbs: 37g
Sugar: 13.6g
Fat: 18.4g
Saturated fat: 7.4g
Fibre: 7.5g
Salt: 2.65g

64

HOT HALLOUMI WITH CRUNCHY COUSCOUS
(Per Serving)

Kcals: 618
Protein: 34g
Carbs: 31.7g
Sugar: 14.7g
Fat: 38.6g
Saturated fat: 20.7g
Fibre: 3.6g
Salt: 4.77g

66

NUTRITIONAL INFORMATION

PASTA PLEASE

PEA PESTO PASTA WITH PANCETTA
(Per Serving)

Kcals: 659
Protein: 30.5g
Carbs: 63.9g
Sugar: 8.7g
Fat: 28.9g
Saturated fat: 7g
Fibre: 10.5g
Salt: 1.77g

70

STORECUPBOARD SPAGHETTI
(Per Serving)

Kcals: 537
Protein: 32.2g
Carbs: 69.9g
Sugar: 10.2g
Fat: 12.9g
Saturated fat: 2.2g
Fibre: 5.5g
Salt: 3.63g

72

CAULI MAC & CHEESE
(Per Serving)

Kcals: 859
Protein: 41.9g
Carbs: 82g
Sugar: 14.2g
Fat: 39.5g
Saturated fat: 23.7g
Fibre: 4.4g
Salt: 2.09g

74

15-MIN FLORENTINE CHICKEN PASTA
(Per Serving)

Kcals: 711
Protein: 61g
Carbs: 47.6g
Sugar: 5.5g
Fat: 29.6g
Saturated fat: 12.7g
Fibre: 5.6g
Salt: 2.08g

76

GARLIC BREAD SPAGHETTI
(Per Serving)

Kcals: 671
Protein: 16.2g
Carbs: 72.6g
Sugar: 7g
Fat: 33.7g
Saturated fat: 15.7g
Fibre: 6.1g
Salt: 1.31g

78

ONE-PAN LASAGNE
(Per Serving)

Kcals: 732g
Protein: 43.7g
Carbs: 60g
Sugar: 15.7g
Fat: 33.4g
Saturated fat: 14.8g
Fibre: 7.7g
Salt: 0.85g

80

15-MINUTE 'BLT' PASTA
(Per Serving)

Kcals: 780
Protein: 28.9g
Carbs: 56g
Sugar: 6.1g
Fat: 47.9g
Saturated fat: 28.1g
Fibre: 4.1g
Salt: 2.24g

82

ONE-POT LAMB ORZO
(Per Serving)

Kcals: 597
Protein: 39.2g
Carbs: 48.9g
Sugar: 6.1g
Fat: 25.2g
Saturated fat: 12g
Fibre: 5.2g
Salt: 3.2g

84

CRISPY GNOCCHI WITH BACON
(Per Serving)

Kcals: 759
Protein: 26.6g
Carbs: 85.5g
Sugar: 7.4g
Fat: 33.9g
Saturated fat: 15.2g
Fibre: 7g
Salt: 3.78g

86

20-MINUTE BEEF STROGANOFF PASTA
(Per Serving)

Kcals: 772
Protein: 41.3g
Carbs: 59.8g
Sugar: 6.7g
Fat: 39.9g
Saturated fat: 19.1g
Fibre: 3.5g
Salt: 2.81g

88

SAUSAGE SPAGHETTI WITH SPINACH
(Per Serving)

Kcals: 778
Protein: 33.4g
Carbs: 72.5g
Sugar: 15.5g
Fat: 37.3g
Saturated fat: 14g
Fibre: 9.2g
Salt: 1.8g

90

15-MINUTE PAPRIKA CHICKEN PASTA
(Per Serving)

Kcals: 615
Protein: 51.2g
Carbs: 39.5g
Sugar: 7.7g
Fat: 26.8g
Saturated fat: 13.6g
Fibre: 4.9g
Salt: 0.94g

92

FAMILY FAVOURITES & FAKEAWAYS

CHEAT'S TORTILLA PIZZAS
(Per Serving)

Kcals: 228
Protein: 11.1g
Carbs: 22g
Sugar: 2.7g
Fat: 10g
Saturated fat: 6.2g
Fibre: 2.4g
Salt: 1.1g

96

PEANUT PORK NOODLES
(Per Serving)

Kcals: 821
Protein: 38.9g
Carbs: 37g
Sugar: 12.4g
Fat: 55.5g
Saturated fat: 15g
Fibre: 8.5g
Salt: 4.23g

98

COCONUT CURRIED SALMON
(Per Serving)

Kcals: 559
Protein: 31.8g
Carbs: 15.2g
Sugar: 10g
Fat: 39.9g
Saturated fat: 18.4g
Fibre: 5.9g
Salt: 1.82g

100

POT PIE IN A PINCH
(Per Serving)

Kcals: 723g
Protein: 52.7g
Carbs: 53.5g
Sugar: 13.6g
Fat: 31.2g
Saturated fat: 13.4g
Fibre: 8.7g
Salt: 0.48g

102

CRUNCHY CUTLETS
(Per Serving)

Kcals: 470
Protein: 32.1g
Carbs: 14.1g
Sugar: 1g
Fat: 31.7g
Saturated fat: 9.9g
Fibre: 1.4g
Salt: 0.54g

104

WARM WALDORF POTATOES
(Per Serving)

Kcals: 214
Protein: 5g
Carbs: 26.2g
Sugar: 9g
Fat: 9g
Saturated fat: 1g
Fibre: 4.5g
Salt: 0.07g

106

CHEEKY CHOPPED SALAD
(Per Serving)

Kcals: 126
Protein: 1.5g
Carbs: 4.7g
Sugar: 4.3g
Fat: 11g
Saturated fat: 1.7g
Fibre: 1.7g
Salt: 0.16g

106

MINTY SMASHED AVOCADOS
(Per Serving)

Kcals: 150
Protein: 1.6g
Carbs: 2g
Sugar: 0.9g
Fat: 14.2g
Saturated fat: 3g
Fibre: 3.8g
Salt: 0.18g

107

QUICK COLCANNON
(Per Serving)

Kcals: 273
Protein: 6.7g
Carbs: 42.4g
Sugar: 4.3g
Fat: 7.2g
Saturated fat: 4g
Fibre: 6.3g
Salt: 0.25g

107

STICKY GINGER PORK
(Per Serving)

Kcals: 511
Protein: 31.9g
Carbs: 58.9g
Sugar: 16g
Fat: 15.8g
Saturated fat: 5.1g
Fibre: 2.3g
Salt: 2.34g

108

NUTRITIONAL INFORMATION

SHEET-PAN STEAK FAJITAS
(Per Serving)
Kcals: 626
Protein: 43.7g
Carbs: 53.3g
Sugar: 8g
Fat: 22.9g
Saturated fat: 7.1g
Fibre: 11.3g
Salt: 2.75g

110

HAWAIIAN-STYLE PORK
(Per Serving)
Kcals: 456
Protein: 34.7g
Carbs: 52.3g
Sugar: 11.6g
Fat: 11g
Saturated fat: 2.5g
Fibre: 4.1g
Salt: 0.63g

112

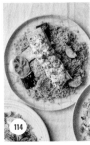

GARLIC FETA LOADED SALMON
(Per Serving)
Kcals: 750
Protein: 45.3g
Carbs: 51.6g
Sugar: 8.3g
Fat: 39.3g
Saturated fat: 11.9g
Fibre: 4.8g
Salt: 2.47g

114

LAZY LAMB TAGINE
(Per Serving)
Kcals: 468
Protein: 32.7g
Carbs: 32.7g
Sugar: 8.3g
Fat: 21.5g
Saturated fat: 8.2g
Fibre: 5g
Salt: 1.01g

116

NO-STIR CHORIZO RISOTTO
(Per Serving)
Kcals: 761
Protein: 30.7g
Carbs: 74.6g
Sugar: 11.5g
Fat: 36.2g
Saturated fat: 17.3g
Fibre: 6.9g
Salt: 4.55g

118

SAUSAGE & MASH WITH A SECRET
(Per Serving)
Kcals: 906
Protein: 24.4g
Carbs: 96.1g
Sugar: 21.1g
Fat: 43.3g
Saturated fat: 17.7g
Fibre: 17g
Salt: 3.51g

120

FRIDAY NIGHT FRIED RICE
(Per Serving)
Kcals: 387
Protein: 31.2g
Carbs: 48.5g
Sugar: 6.1g
Fat: 6.1g
Saturated fat: 1g
Fibre: 7g
Salt: 2.77g

122

HOTPOT IN A HURRY
(Per Serving)
Kcals: 613
Protein: 33.2g
Carbs: 59.4g
Sugar: 13.5g
Fat: 25g
Saturated fat: 9.3g
Fibre: 8.5g
Salt: 2.15g

124

STICKY GAMMON STEAKS
(Per Serving)
Kcals: 312
Protein: 35.1g
Carbs: 3.5g
Sugar: 3.4g
Fat: 17.4g
Saturated fat: 5.3g
Fibre: 0.2g
Salt: 4.41g

126

FISH PIE IN A FLASH
(Per Serving)
Kcals: 506
Protein: 47.8g
Carbs: 38g
Sugar: 10.9g
Fat: 16.9g
Saturated fat: 5.1g
Fibre: 5.3g
Salt: 1.92g

128

MINTY GREENS
(Per Serving)
Kcals: 170
Protein: 5g
Carbs: 10.1g
Sugar: 9.8g
Fat: 11.4g
Saturated fat: 6.7g
Fibre: 7.1g
Salt: 0.49g

129

FULLY LOADED FISH NAAN
(Per Serving)
Kcals: 719
Protein: 38.5g
Carbs: 86.8g
Sugar: 15.7g
Fat: 20.1g
Saturated fat: 2.7g
Fibre: 9.3g
Salt: 1.75g

130

BROCCOLI & BACON BAKE
(Per Serving)

Kcals: 566
Protein: 28.7g
Carbs: 46.6g
Sugar: 10.3g
Fat: 28.1g
Saturated fat: 14.4g
Fibre: 6.2g
Salt: 2.49g

132

ONE-POT CAJUN-STYLE CHICKEN & RICE
(Per Serving)

Kcals: 483
Protein: 32.5g
Carbs: 48.8g
Sugar: 7.2g
Fat: 16.4g
Saturated fat: 4.1g
Fibre: 5.1g
Salt: 1.35g

134

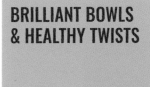

BRILLIANT BOWLS & HEALTHY TWISTS

SALMON BITE BOWLS
(Per Serving)

Kcals: 762
Protein: 33.1g
Carbs: 64.2g
Sugar: 6.9g
Fat: 40.3g
Saturated fat: 6.3g
Fibre: 5.1g
Salt: 0.57g

138

15-MINUTE FISH TACOS
(Per Serving)

Kcals: 516
Protein: 34.1g
Carbs: 55.4g
Sugar: 13.9g
Fat: 15.4g
Saturated fat: 4.4g
Fibre: 10g
Salt: 2.4g

140

BUILD-YOUR-OWN BURRITO BOWLS
(Per Serving)

Kcals: 801
Protein: 46.1g
Carbs: 93.5g
Sugar: 9.3g
Fat: 24.4g
Saturated fat: 4g
Fibre: 11g
Salt: 2.05g

142

BACON & CORN CHOWDER
(Per Serving)

Kcals: 543
Protein: 21.1g
Carbs: 69.7g
Sugar: 17.2g
Fat: 17.8g
Saturated fat: 5.6g
Fibre: 9.4g
Salt: 3.37g

144

GREEK CHICKEN BOWLS
(Per Serving)

Kcals: 824
Protein: 54.4g
Carbs: 74.8g
Sugar: 9g
Fat: 33g
Saturated fat: 14.2g
Fibre: 4.7g
Salt: 2.97g

146

NAKED BURRITO RICE
(Per Serving)

Kcals: 732
Protein: 40.3g
Carbs: 77.5g
Sugar: 6.9g
Fat: 25.2g
Saturated fat: 9.4g
Fibre: 7.9g
Salt: 0.73g

148

MOROCCAN-STYLE CHICKEN
(Per Serving)

Kcals: 593
Protein: 46.5g
Carbs: 57.2g
Sugar: 13.5g
Fat: 18.2g
Saturated fat: 2.5g
Fibre: 7.3g
Salt: 1.47g

150

HONEY & LIME TURKEY NOODLE BOWL
(Per Serving)

Kcals: 496
Protein: 34.3g
Carbs: 71g
Sugar: 27.6g
Fat: 7g
Saturated fat: 1.2g
Fibre: 3.1g
Salt: 0.97g

152

CRISPY PESTO COD
(Per Serving)

Kcals: 230
Protein: 30.7g
Carbs: 2.3g
Sugar: 1.6g
Fat: 10.5g
Saturated fat: 2.2g
Fibre: 2.2g
Salt: 1.86g

154

NUTRITIONAL INFORMATION

STICKY TURKEY TACOS
(Per Serving)

Kcals: 686
Protein: 47.1g
Carbs: 59.4g
Sugar: 10.3g
Fat: 24.7g
Saturated fat: 9.4g
Fibre: 9.6g
Salt: 1.49g

156

BALSAMIC POTATOES
(Per Serving)

Kcals: 235
Protein: 5.1g
Carbs: 33.5g
Sugar: 7.5g
Fat: 7.4g
Saturated fat: 1.1g
Fibre: 5.9g
Salt: 1.46g

158

GARLIC & HERB MASH
(Per Serving)

Kcals: 330
Protein: 9.1g
Carbs: 41.8g
Sugar: 3.8g
Fat: 13g
Saturated fat: 7.9g
Fibre: 4.5g
Salt: 0.53g

158

ZESTY LIME SLAW
(Per Serving)

Kcals: 231
Protein: 2.9g
Carbs: 15.1g
Sugar: 15.1g
Fat: 16.9g
Saturated fat: 2.8g
Fibre: 3.1g
Salt: 0.27g

159

SPEEDY SWEET POTATO FRIES
(Per Serving)

Kcals: 297
Protein: 3.3g
Carbs: 49.8g
Sugar: 13.9g
Fat: 7.7g
Saturated fat: 1.3g
Fibre: 7.8g
Salt: 0.4g

159

QUICK TUNA & PEA PATTIES
(Per Serving)

Kcals: 325
Protein: 22.6g
Carbs: 25g
Sugar: 7.8g
Fat: 14.5g
Saturated fat: 5g
Fibre: 4.3g
Salt: 0.73g

160

PARMESAN-CRUSTED COD
(Per Serving)

Kcals: 242
Protein: 26.4g
Carbs: 11.3g
Sugar: 1.2g
Fat: 10.4g
Saturated fat: 2.7g
Fibre: 0.5g
Salt: 0.71g

162

CRISPY SALMON W. PINEAPPLE SALSA
(Per Serving)

Kcals: 657
Protein: 33.6g
Carbs: 78.6g
Sugar: 19.3g
Fat: 22.2g
Saturated fat: 3.9g
Fibre: 3.9g
Salt: 1.27g

164

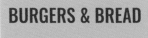

BURGERS & BREAD

ZESTY LAMB PITTAS
(Per Serving)

Kcals: 707
Protein: 40.2g
Carbs: 59.6g
Sugar: 6.5g
Fat: 32.4g
Saturated fat: 9.8g
Fibre: 8g
Salt: 1.92g

168

SLOPPY JOE SANDWICHES
(Per Serving)

Kcals: 498
Protein: 42.1g
Carbs: 41.4g
Sugar: 12.7g
Fat: 17.5g
Saturated fat: 8.6g
Fibre: 3.7g
Salt: 2.35g

170

CHEESY CORN
(Per Serving)

Kcals: 177
Protein: 4.9g
Carbs: 6.5g
Sugar: 2.4g
Fat: 13.7g
Saturated fat: 2.1g
Fibre: 3.6g
Salt: 0.37g

172

**ROASTED AUBERGINE
SALAD**
(Per Serving)

Kcals: 130
Protein: 4.2g
Carbs: 5.6g
Sugar: 5.1g
Fat: 9.2g
Saturated fat: 4.0g
Fibre: 3.8g
172 **Salt:** 1.52g

COWBOY CAVIAR
(Per Serving)

Kcals: 193
Protein: 11.6g
Carbs: 27.3g
Sugar: 9.3g
Fat: 1.9g
Saturated fat: 0.4g
Fibre: 9.4g
173 **Salt:** 0.33g

WEDGE SALAD
(Per Serving)

Kcals: 210
Protein: 5.8g
Carbs: 3.7g
Sugar: 3.1g
Fat: 18.9g
Saturated fat: 3.9g
Fibre: 1g
173 **Salt:** 0.87g

**BARBECUE CHICKEN
BURGERS**
(Per Serving)

Kcals: 618
Protein: 47.6g
Carbs: 35.5g
Sugar: 14.9g
Fat: 31.6g
Saturated fat: 11.2g
Fibre: 1.7g
174 **Salt:** 3.02g

**SPEEDY SMASH
BURGERS**
(Per Serving)

Kcals: 451
Protein: 37.2g
Carbs: 27.5g
Sugar: 6.4g
Fat: 21g
Saturated fat: 5.4g
Fibre: 1.9g
176 **Salt:** 2.55g

**LOADED SAUSAGE
SUBS**
(Per Serving)

Kcals: 597
Protein: 23.2g
Carbs: 43.8g
Sugar: 13g
Fat: 34.8g
Saturated fat: 13.4g
Fibre: 6.7g
178 **Salt:** 2.09g

**PORK & APPLE
BURGERS**
(Per Serving)

Kcals: 451
Protein: 29.2g
Carbs: 25.3g
Sugar: 4.9g
Fat: 25.2g
Saturated fat: 6.7g
Fibre: 3.1g
180 **Salt:** 0.81g

PESTO POTATO SALAD
(Per Serving)

Kcals: 424
Protein: 8.9g
Carbs: 30.2g
Sugar: 6g
Fat: 28.3g
Saturated fat: 3.9g
Fibre: 6.5g
182 **Salt:** 0.25g

**SPICED CAULIFLOWER
SALAD**
(Per Serving)

Kcals: 145
Protein: 5.7g
Carbs: 9.6g
Sugar: 7g
Fat: 9g
Saturated fat: 1.7g
Fibre: 2.5g
182 **Salt:** 0.28g

**CRUNCHY PEANUT
SALAD**
(Per Serving)

Kcals: 242
Protein: 9.3g
Carbs: 17.9g
Sugar: 16.1g
Fat: 13.7g
Saturated fat: 3g
Fibre: 4.7g
183 **Salt:** 1.58g

RAINBOW COLESLAW
(Per Serving)

Kcals: 303
Protein: 5.2g
Carbs: 9.5g
Sugar: 8.5g
Fat: 25.9g
Saturated fat: 3.8g
Fibre: 4.7g
183 **Salt:** 0.29g

**CHICKEN TIKKA-STYLE
NAAN BURGERS**
(Per Serving)

Kcals: 513
Protein: 38.9g
Carbs: 38.6g
Sugar: 15.9g
Fat: 21.6g
Saturated fat: 5.4g
Fibre: 5.4g
184 **Salt:** 2.27g

NUTRITIONAL INFORMATION

STICKY PEANUT STRIPS
(Per Serving)

Kcals: 416
Protein: 41.3g
Carbs: 22.1g
Sugar: 6.2g
Fat: 17.5g
Saturated fat: 5.4g
Fibre: 2.6g
Salt: 2.19g

186

WEEKEND TREATS

IVY'S CHEESE SCONES
(Per Serving)

Kcals: 438
Protein: 14.9g
Carbs: 48.4g
Sugar: 2.2g
Fat: 20g
Saturated fat: 12g
Fibre: 2.6g
Salt: 1.69g

190

OATMEAL CHUNK COOKIES
(Per Serving)

Kcals: 219
Protein: 3.2g
Carbs: 28g
Sugar: 15.6g
Fat: 10.1g
Saturated fat: 5.8g
Fibre: 1.6g
Salt: 0.13g

192

CHOCOLATE BROWNIE COOKIES
(Per Serving)

Kcals: 301
Protein: 4g
Carbs: 33.8g
Sugar: 21.4g
Fat: 16.4g
Saturated fat: 9.9g
Fibre: 1.4g
Salt: 0.4g

194

BISCUIT TIN TIFFIN
(Per Serving)

Kcals: 406
Protein: 4.5g
Carbs: 38.4g
Sugar: 27.3g
Fat: 25.5g
Saturated fat: 13.6g
Fibre: 2.5g
Salt: 0.44g

195

CHEAT'S DANISH PASTRIES
(Per Serving)

Kcals: 340
Protein: 4.1g
Carbs: 50.4g
Sugar: 36.6g
Fat: 13g
Saturated fat: 6.1g
Fibre: 2.6g
Salt: 0.45g

196

STRAWBERRY SHORTCAKES
(Per Serving)

Kcals: 533
Protein: 10.2g
Carbs: 61.4g
Sugar: 15.4g
Fat: 26.7g
Saturated fat: 15.9g
Fibre: 3.3g
Salt: 0.57g

198

SALTED PRETZEL FUDGE
(Per Serving)

Kcals: 107
Protein: 2g
Carbs: 14.5g
Sugar: 12g
Fat: 4.5g
Saturated fat: 2.7g
Fibre: 0.4g
Salt: 0.20g

200

PEANUT BUTTER & JELLY COOKIES
(Per Serving)

Kcals: 326
Protein: 9.1g
Carbs: 33.2g
Sugar: 31.3g
Fat: 16.9g
Saturated fat: 4.2g
Fibre: 2.1g
Salt: 0.31g

202

LEMON & RASPBERRY MUFFINS
(Per Serving)

Kcals: 256
Protein: 3.2g
Carbs: 23.9g
Sugar: 14.9g
Fat: 11.8g
Saturated fat: 7g
Fibre: 0.6g
Salt: 0.17g

204

TOFFEE POPCORN ROCKY ROAD
(Per Serving)

Kcals: 315
Protein: 3g
Carbs: 33g
Sugar: 28.2g
Fat: 18.7g
Saturated fat: 10.4g
Fibre: 1.8g
Salt: 0.09g

206

INDEX

INDEX

INDEX

ACKNOWLEDGEMENTS

The biggest thank you of all thank yous goes to YOU. If you've made one of my recipes, clicked like on a video or shared one of my posts with a friend, I am so grateful as this book wouldn't exist without you.

If you're juggling work, children, school pick up, homework, trying to be healthy, be a good friend, be a good parent, and by dinner time it all feels just… too much. I see you, I feel you, I am you and I wrote this book for you. I hope these recipes genuinely make your life a little easier.

Mum – thank you for all the hours you spent in the kitchen with me as I was growing up, so patiently encouraging me. I'm sure I wouldn't be here, doing this job I love, if you hadn't.

Debbie, Miranda, Claire – I couldn't have written this book without you and all the amazing work you have put into helping make Taming Twins what it is this year. THANK YOU!

Zoë – thank you for our endless voice notes, for listening to my ideas with such enthusiasm and giving me the clarity of your relentless pep talks. Your friendship makes me a better human.

Anna – thank you for being there for the good times and the bad and for dancing with me until 2am at every opportunity. As well as being the best friend a girl could want you've been right there with me working on all of this, too. Patiently adjusting a parsley leaf in every video or photo until it was JUST RIGHT, celebrating my successes and wanting this book to be every bit as brilliant as I did. Thank you so much my darling friend.

Naomi – thank you for loving me even through my terrible fringe years and for all the veggie (and cheese!) inspiration.

Emma – thank you for always making me feel less alone in this online world and for your words of wisdom, friendship and support when I've needed it the most.

Nic – thank you for all the recipe book 'what not to do' advice right from the start. I hope I've made something you'll love to have on your shelf.

Mark and Louise – thank you for inspiring me with your Instagram worthy feasts for the last 20 years, before Instagram even existed!

Dave – thank you for being even more excited than me when I got this book deal and for all those years moaning about my cooking to keep me on my toes.

Laurie – thank you so much for holding my hand through this adventure.

Lydia – thank you so much for trusting my idea for this book and all of your help and support in making it a reality.

Imogen, Hattie, Hugo and Sophia – thank you for coming into my life and bringing with you so much laughter and joy. You are the family I never ever expected to have and the family I cannot believe my luck that I ended up with. I am so grateful for you all.

Dem – you are my inspiration. People say that thing 'I couldn't have done it without you' but I really could not have even thought about being able to do this without you stepping up in every possible way. You've taught me what it means to be fearless in life and love. Thank you for everything.

And finally… to George and Harriet. None of this would have happened if you hadn't been there, throwing your fish pie at me, all those years ago. Thank you for all your love and encouragement. I hope that when you see this book in the shops, you'll be half as proud of me as I am of you, every single day.